MW00603835

Lynne,

Thanks for
your kind hosting and
support!

Laura Bini

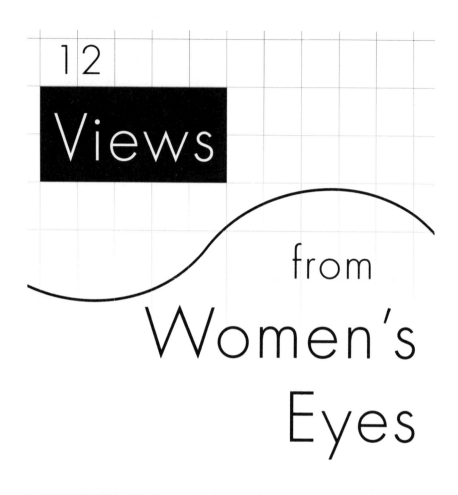

12 Views from Women's Eyes

managing the new majority

Laura Ricci, M.B.A.

with George Wilkerson, Ph.D.

$\mathbb{R}^3$

Box 26249
Austin, Texas 78755
Phone: (512) 349-2495
Book orders: 1-800-953-6755
Book orders by E-mail: http://www.R-3.com/bookorder.htm

Copyright © 1997 by Laura Ricci

All rights reserved. No part of this book may be reproduced or used in any form or by any means, electronic or mechanical, without permission from the Publisher. Reproduction of up to 100 words for the purposes of published review is acceptable to the publisher with notice by mailing the a copy of the published review to R³, P.O. Box 26249, Austin, Texas, 78755.

First Printing 1997

LCCN 97-091622

Library of Congress Cataloging-in-Publication Data

Ricci, Laura
12 Views From Women's Eyes, Managing the New Majority / Laura Ricci, M.B.A. with George Wilkerson Ph.D.
    p.   cm
Includes illustrations and worksheets.

1. Management: Communication in management
2. Women: Employment
3. Management: Organizational change
4. Women: Communication
5. Management: Organizational effectiveness

ISBN 0-9657399-0-2   97-091622

Printed in the United States of America at Morgan Printing in Austin, Texas

Cover design by Stephen Bright
Page Design by Terry Sherrell

From women's eyes this doctrine I derive:
They sparkle still the right Promethean fire;
They are the books, the arts, the academes,
That show, contain, and nourish all the world.

— William Shakespeare
Love's Labour's Lost

CONTENTS

Preface

"*The case for integrating diversity into our corporate culture is strong. First, the future employment base will be made up largely of minorities, including Hispanics, Asians, African-Americans and women. If a company is going to attract the best talent, it must be known that it is culturally diverse and committed to equality. Second, the American customer base is changing: more growth will come from the minority population.*

Because of our changing business environment, companies that do not recognize these principles will be overshadowed by those that do. As a result, these companies will find themselves noncompetitive and ineffective in the next century. No one wants to do business with a company that discriminates."

— Ronald C. Petty
The New York Times
November 16, 1996

Over 40 percent of today's workforce in the United States is female. Their numbers are already significant among the executive, administrative and managerial workforce (42 percent in the 1992 census; that's just four percentage points below the share for all employed persons[1].) And yet, you rarely find them among the high ranking corporate leaders[2]. This is ironic, because those firms which fail to integrate the diverse talents of the female half of the workforce into their organization have cut nearly in half the methods, solutions and benefits that are available to them. As the new millennium approaches and the balance shifts, the irony will be all the more obvious. By the turn of the century, women in the workforce will outnumber the men.

The recommendations and techniques in this book are aimed at giving managers the tools to tap into the power of the new majority and retain the benefits that men have already brought to the workplace. While we have put most of what we say into gender-specific terms, we recognize that not all men operate from a purely masculine perspective or that all women act in a feminine way. We're not into stereotyping; we're into changing motivation. We're not into overhauling; we're into awareness. Look around you; watch and listen. If you believe that everyone in your organization ought to work the same way, communicate alike, and approach problems with a single mind-set, this book will do little more than disturb and dismay you. But if you see the value in the diversity that surely exists in your organization and you want to exploit that by applying the best abilities of *everyone,* you may find some helpful ideas here. We encourage you to use what we offer as a way to build an atmosphere where flexibility, respect for diversity, and attention to the important, external matters thrive.

Laura L. Ricci
George J. Wilkerson
1997 Austin, Texas

---

[1]American Demographics June, 1993.

[2]Business Week article on CEOs in America, 1992. The survey found only 3 women among the CEOs of America's 1,000 most valuable publicly held companies.

This book is for the men and women of all gender orientations who have gone into management and understood what "to manage" meant.

— George Wilkerson, Ph.D.

Quoi que vous fassiez, écrasez l'infâme et aimez qui vous aime.

— Voltaire

(Whatever you do, trample down abuses, and love those who love you.)

— Laura Ricci, M.B.A.

CHAPTER 1

Anticipating the Critical Mass

Eleven Tips on getting more efficiency out of women employees:

1) Pick young married women. They usually have more of a sense of responsibility than their unmarried sisters, they're less likely to be flirtatious, they need the work or they wouldn't be doing it, they still have the pep and interest to work hard and to deal with the public efficiently.

2) When you have to use older women, try to get ones who have worked outside the home at some time in their lives. Older women who have never contacted the public have a hard time adapting themselves and are inclined to be cantankerous and fussy. It's always well to impress upon older women the importance of friendliness and courtesy.

3) *General experience indicates that "husky" girls—those who are just a little on the heavy side—are more even tempered and efficient than their underweight sisters.*

4) *Retain a physician to give each woman you hire a special physical examination—one covering female conditions. This step not only protects the property against the possibilities of lawsuit, but reveals whether the employee-to-be has any female weaknesses which would make her mentally or physically unfit for the job.*

5) *Stress at the outset the importance of time—the fact that a minute or two lost here and there makes serious inroads on schedules. Until this point is gotten across, service is likely to be slowed up.*

6) *Give the female employee a definite daylong schedule of duties so that they'll keep busy without bothering the management for instructions every few minutes. Numerous properties say that women make excellent workers when they have their jobs cut out for them, but that they lack initiative in finding work themselves.*

7) *Whenever possible, let the inside employee change from one job to another at some time during the day. Women are inclined to be less nervous and happier with change.*

8) *Give every girl an adequate number of rest periods during the day. You have to make some allowances for feminine psychology. A girl has more confidence and is more efficient if she can keep her hair tidied, apply fresh lipstick and wash her hands several times a day.*

9) *Be tactful when issuing instructions or in making criticisms. Women are often sensitive, they can't shrug off harsh words the way men do. Never ridicule a woman—it breaks her spirit and cuts off her efficiency.*

10) *Be reasonably considerate about using strong language around women. Even though a girl's husband or father may swear vociferously, she'll grow to dislike a place of business where she hears too much of this.*

11) Get enough size variety in operators uniforms so that each girl can have a proper fit. This point can't be stressed too strongly as a means of keeping women happy.

The excerpt above, from the July 1943 issue of *Mass Transportation*, was written for male supervisors of women in the work force at Western Properties during World War II. Of course, no self-respecting manager (of either gender) would issue such guidelines today. And yet, we are at last willing to recognize that men and women **are** different and should be dealt with differently.

We willingly recognize that *Men are from Mars and Women are From Venus[1]*. Now that the percentage of women in the work force is approaching the level of a critical mass, it's past time to consider how to deal with **both** genders in ways that produce greater efficiency, productivity, and job satisfaction.

The Henry Higgins Strategy:
Act Like a Man

Over the years, many firms developed successful strategies for managing the talents of their employees —the men, that is. So it only seemed right that as women made inroads into the corporate world, the strategy they had to adopt was simple: *act like a man*. That worked for some women, but many others were offended by that approach and rejected it. And rightly so. How would a man feel in that position? Told that he must act like a woman to get ahead in an organization, we know what most men would say, and it's not very polite.

[1] *Men Are from Mars, Women Are from Venus: A Practical Guide for Improving Communication and Getting What You Want in Your Relationships*, by John Gray, Harpercollins, June 1,1992

The *act like a man* strategy remained in vogue even as the women's movement gained momentum. The publically advertised position was total equality. Recognizing the differences that were patently obvious was verboten. But now the pendulum has swung back. Admitting the obvious, that women are different from men, is no longer politically incorrect. Research shows and practical experience confirms that women and men approach problems, communicate, and manage differently and it's finally all right to say so.

Even more important: many aspects of the modern marketplace *favor* the natural talents of women over men. Recognizing that and adding it to what we already know about managing men is what will mark the difference between the corporate winners and losers in the 21st century.

Strength Is Not Always Measured by Muscle

Team building training is common in many modern organizations. Workshops aimed at building teams are based on the proven fact that greater success is possible when you exploit the different talents within a team. For women, this concept is no surprise, but for men, it's often a revelation.

Because women don't usually have the competitive aggressiveness that is more common to men, the men in an organization stand more likely to grab an opportunity and wrestle it to the ground. Businesses able to recognize the value of both approaches and capitalize on them double their opportunities for success. But, whatever their reasons, any business which chooses to discount the talents of a portion of their workforce reduces the possibility of success by an equal amount.

Double opportunity for success
Expand the pool of talent contributing to success

Company A   Company B   Company C

☐ Manages Men well
▨ Focuses on Feminine management
■ Opportunity for both men and women to excel

Creating a Gender Free
Problem Solving Corporate Culture

The real world is neither consistent nor homogenized. And yet, the leaders in many organizations want information to come back to them in a consistent, homogenized form. They expend enormous amounts of energy trying to make their employees behave in a common fashion. They have missed the point that those who are most flexible win. Chinese philosophers, Italian strategists, German military leaders, and modern Neurolinguistic Psychologists all recognize the advantages of flexibility. The only ones who succeed are those flexible enough to accept different solutions for different problems (and try again when the first one doesn't work).

```
------------------------- Message -------------------------
To: Laura Ricci
From: George Wilkerson
Subject: The male ego


Laura-

I can't help but think of some of the men I've worked for who
will read this and think you're saying they should give up
their masculinity if they want to have a successful "culture."
How do you deal with the fragile male ego in all of this?

------------------------- Message -------------------------
To: George Wilkerson
From: Laura Ricci
Subject: The male ego


Hmmm. Actually the point is just the opposite. The traditional
male gender methods are worthwhile and need to be groomed to
continue succeeding.  That voice should not be muted.

On the other hand, folks who work from the female gender role
have valuable input to offer.  Those managers who welcome and
harness the resources of both genders have twice the power as
those who ignore half the suggestions available.

Some managers do this well, and they have great advantage over
those who don't.  Is flexibility a threat to masculinity? Not
at all.
```

Most firms are complex. They have complex problems and the best solution for each of those problems varies. The style needed to get there varies as well. If your firm's corporate culture is strictly a male culture requiring that everyone adopt the male mind set, the women will submerge their natural inclinations or leave the firm. When your hiring practices establish a pool where only those who can be successful must emulate a male culture, few women will be in that pool. If you seek homogeneous talent because you want to be sure your employees will "fit in," the cost of solving your problems will be higher. Without the broad base of gender free problem-solving, you cut off your access to all of the possibilities; you lose the ability to quickly solve a wider range of problems. That's why success is endangered by not using the advantages of both genders to lower the cost and speed up solving problems.

In the same way as there are firms with a male culture, there are some firms which pride themselves on having a more feminine management style. Their hiring practices cull out candidates from the other side of the coin, eliminating those who operate from a traditional male-oriented structure. In both instances, the cost of homogenization is high. In the future, those firms able to attract and exploit the talents of men *and* women, who select candidates from that larger pool of talent, who solicit the participation of all of the workforce, and who work from a management model which is gender free, will stand out as the leaders.

Shifting the Focus from Internal to External

One corporate manager gave out this formula for managing resources: *Spend 40 percent of your energy pleasing your supervisor, 50 percent*

---

[2] CYA—"Cover Your Ass"—a quaint bit of slang referring to the need to avoid responsibility (i.e., blame), documenting everything you do, and being able to plead innocence when the manure hits the fan—in sharp contrast to an environment in which the focus is on solving problems and getting the job done.

6

```
------------------------ Message ------------------------
To: Laura Ricci
From: George Wilkerson
Subject: Reorganizing people out

That manager you mentioned sounds like one of mine.  Another
trick he had was to use a reorganization as a way to get rid of
people.  Rather than axing someone, he simply announced a
reorganization in which that person's job conveniently
disappeared.


------------------------ Message ------------------------
To: George Wilkerson
From: Laura Ricci
Subject: Reorgng people out

Chicken.  In an atmosphere of litigousness, I know managers have
to be careful what they say — but to say nothing and surprise
folks with a summary dismissal is just chicken.  The anger I've
heard is usually aimed at these kinds of managers.

Most folks I know have a difficult time dealing with a layoff,
but this kind of tactic denies simple dignity to this manager's
victim.  The victim is better off out of such an organization.

The manager gets a lesson later on.  Most of the good people
learn the manager's tactics and make their own plans
accordingly.  It's tough keeping good people when you treat them
like hired help.
```

pleasing the people you work with, and give the remaining 10 percent to solving customer problems. This is a recipe for disaster; the atmosphere in his company is strictly CYA[2]. Rather than focusing on what's in front of them and solving problems, his employees focus on what's behind them and keeping that part of their anatomy covered.

That manager didn't understand that the focus for growing a successful business is external, on the customer, the competition, and the changing marketplace. The more energy spent on internal matters (how to emulate your superiors, how to "fit in" with your peers, how to work within "the system") the less energy you have to focus on those things that make a difference. The only way an organization can clearly see what's happening in those areas outside of the organization is to have everyone *in* the organization focused on what's going on *out*side of it. Combine this focus with the different viewpoints promoted by a gender free management and you'll be astonished at the increase in understanding, the number of good solutions you find, and the increase in your company's success.

If your firm suffers from internal skirmishes, how much energy is left for the real challenge — outside your door — meeting the marketplace?

Causing Fundamental Changes

The risky part of causing a change is that unintended changes can occur because of unanticipated motivations. The unanticipated motivation resulting from affirmative action was the resentment and ultimate backlash from those who found themselves the subject of reverse discrimination. If you want a fundamental change to occur, you must first change people's motivations. People respond precisely to the motivations presented.[3] Changes must be balanced against their costs. Reorganizing brings some good, but it also causes some disruption. Picture the organization as a scale, with opposing and supporting forces balanced on each side of the fulcrum. The goal is to gently rearrange the forces so that we take away the negative attributes while keeping the positive attributes. Measures which are too drastic or heavy-handed cause chaos rather than improvement. Change is rarely drastic, but it can seem drastic to those within the organization.

And Our Point is...

Lest there be any confusion, the techniques and recommendations we make are aimed at changing motivation; we're not promoting an

---

[3] As taught by Andrea Stalsworth Rice, LMSW-ACP, LPC.LMFT, Founder, The Institute of NLP, Austin, TX.

[4] Entrepreneurial start-ups often require conformity to control the explosive addition of manpower (over 20 percent per year) and avoid dissolving into chaos as the organization defines itself. However, once the second phase (growth and competition) begins, a management transition must occur. At that point, as competitors get a bead on your organization and take aim, flexibility becomes key.

```
------------------------- Message -------------------------
To: Laura Ricci
From: George Wilkerson
Subject: The S Word

What about sexual harassment? I notice the S-E-X word isn't
mentioned here anywhere. Is that because it's been beaten to
death already or don't you think it's a factor?

------------------------- Message -------------------------
To: George Wilkerson
From: Laura Ricci
Subject: The S Word

We're not talking about sex here, but about gender differences.
There are some women who have modeled themselves successfully
on the male model, just as there are men who are uncomfortable
with some parts of the male culture.

Most of us can identify with the models as distinct from each
other. The interesting thing is to see how the combination of
the two styles can be very powerful in the workplace.

A great story I heard last week was of a woman whose father
bemoaned losing money in the stock market on a Women's clothing
chain. His daughter was miffed that he only used the counsel
of his stockbroker (also male) who presented the fabulous
earnings of the past 5 years. The daughter, her mother, and
their friends had been enthusiastic patrons until a few years
ago when the merchandise changed and none of them shop there
anymore. Her father wasn't able to be flexible and use the
input from the female gender along with the input from the male
gender. Would have been a great chance to sell short!
```

overhaul. If your organization needs everyone to concentrate on working in the same way, communicating and approaching problems in the same way, this book will only disturb and dismay you[4]. But if you want everyone in your organization to bring their best abilities to bear on the problems you face now and are bound to face in the future, this book can help you build an atmosphere where flexibility, respect for diversity, and attention to the important, external matters thrive.

AS A RULE:

- **Recognize the natural talents of women.**
  And add it to what you already know about managing men

- **Establish a cross-gendered hiring pool.**
  Seek heterogeneous talent; the cost of solving your problems will be a lot lower..

- **Shift the Focus from Internal to External.**
  Focus on what's in front of you and on solving external problems.

- **Rearrange forces gently**.
  As you take away the negative attributes, make sure you keep the positive. Avoid drastic or heavy-handed methods.

EXERCISE BREAK

Have you ever met a man who operates from the feminine gender identification? How about a woman who operates from a male gender orientation?

On a piece of paper, draw a line across the top of the page. Label one end "male" and the opposite end "female." Write down the names of five or six co-workers placing each co-worker along the scale between "male" and "female," in regards to the strength of their personal gender identification. Think of each person individually as you place them on the scale.

This exercise gives you a chance to focus on gender identification in your workforce. If you do this, you'll find it's easier to see how to apply the techniques we offer. You should see that there's a good deal of "grey area" and that's why we suggest you consider where someone fits on this scale when selecting techniques, not simply whether they produce testosterone. With a female who registers toward the male end of the scale, you may have success using some male approaches. The results you get might get look something like this:

```
MALE ─────────────────────────────── FEMALE

1.   Tom
2.                                        Nancy
3.                           Joe
4.              Beverly
5.                              Sue Ann
```

This is not about sexuality. It's about gender-related orientation. You're most likely to rank women who are ultra-feminine, tender, motherly at the far end of the scale, toward the female side, while you'd most likely rank men who are ultra-macho, eat nails for breakfast, and hunt moose over their lunch hour at the far end of the scale toward the male side. You should have found the genders mixed somewhat, depending on your workforce. (Just how often do your folks bring moose meat sandwiches for lunch?)

CHAPTER 2

Girls Join In; Guys Join Up

[Voice Mail] *"At the tone, please leave your message."*

Steve: *"Barbara, I've been trying to reach the phone company to find out about adding call forwarding to my phone at home. I can't get through. While you're at the front desk, would you try to get through for me?"*

Barbara: *"Hi Steve. I've arranged to have call forwarding added to your home phone. The installation charge will be $16.50 and the monthly charge will be $6.00."*

Steve: *"Barbara! This is Steve. I got your voice mail...what are you saying?! I never told you to go ahead and INSTALL the service!*

I just wanted to know how much it would cost and whether I could get it in my neighborhood! You can't just take the world into your own hands like that! I'll be writing an incident report on this. More later."

It never dawned on Stephen that Barbara would take what to her was the obvious next step and complete the arrangements. And it never dawned on Barbara that Stephen would be anything but thrilled that she had saved him some time and trouble. The problem was a basic misunderstanding about responsibility. Women assume it, and men resist it.

Who's Responsible (and Who's Not)?

You've got to be aware of the difference between the way men and women handle responsibility. Women take it; men leave it. Woman stay late and take responsibility for seeing to it that the boss's report is safely in the hands of a courier, long after the boss went home because he didn't want to miss dinner. Women are quick to take on other people's problems, ready to charge ahead without *checking with the authorities* first. (And that's why you rarely hear of *female bonding*.)

Men have had to learn to bond to other men because they have learned NOT to take on other people's problems. Most men are taught to *check with the authorities* before *going off half- cocked.* They resist responsibility, so they have to be taught to take it. Army boot camp focuses on tasks which can't be completed successfully without the help of others in the unit. Sometimes the entire unit must finish the task before it's considered complete. All of this is done to instill a sense of responsibility for others in the unit because such responsibility is a necessity for a successful mission.

Would You Mind Watching My Books?

In research performed many times on college campuses, the responsibility difference has been demonstrated repeatedly. The classic study has college students waiting in a long line. They don't know there's a researcher among them. The researcher asks one of the students to watch his or her books for a few minutes. Once the student agrees, the researcher leaves. After a few minutes, Researcher Number Two walks up and takes the books. In every case, female students act to protect the books, attempting to stop Number Two, making some effort to interrupt the apparent theft. And in every case, male students make no attempt to protect the belongings. Men just don't want to be responsible.

The researchers suspect that we're "programmed" by gender to respond differently in order to accomplish basic biological goals. Females may take responsibility easier because the offspring require an overseer, someone who takes responsibility for the children and keeps them safe. Because men must hunt, they avoid responsibilities that could dull their competitive advantage.

```
------------------------ Message ------------------------
To: Laura Ricci
From: George Wilkerson
Subject: Politics

Laura: If we look at politics (i.e. politicians) we can see
some clear examples of the language of non-responsibility.
Sadly enough, the language seems to get adopted by women who
move into the political arena. About eighty percent of
everything that's said by politicians is phrased so that
responsibility is diverted. Isn't it refreshing when someone,
regardless of gender, says "It was my fault?"

------------------------ Message ------------------------
To: George Wilkerson
From: Laura Ricci
Subject: Politics

Ahh yes, politics. What is the current saying? Show business
for less attractive people. And did you notice that women who
take responsibility (Hillary Clinton, Libby Dole) are quite
visible and subject to criticism for being too aggressive, just
like Barbara in our opening story?
```

The implication of this in the workplace is simple. Responsibility itself should be clear, not just the *lines* of responsibility. In the next chapter we address the structure of the organization. Male dominated organizations, which are usually hierarchical, diminish personal responsibility, making it easy to hide from responsibility. The manager who wants to involve both genders needs to make sure that responsibility issues do not go unspoken. Clearly define (or assign) responsibility; don't leave it to the understanding of the employee.

And, If Something Happens?

In recent experiments[1] researchers asked strangers one of three questions: "Would you go to bed with me tonight? Would you come over to my apartment tonight?" or "Would you go out with me tonight?" Over 75 percent of the men said yes when a woman asked them to go to bed. The men were less likely to agree to going to the woman's apartment, and least likely to agree to go out her. The women's responses were just the opposite. None of them agreed to go to bed with a strange man or to his apartment, but they were quite willing to explore opportunities to get to know him. This may reflect some of what's at work when the issue of responsibility comes up. Women are more accustomed to thinking about "consequences."

A woman's greater need to accept responsibility may relate to the possibility of pregnancy. Even our language supports this; uncomfortable pauses, where we feel obliged to speak, are called *pregnant*. The consequences of sex moderate a woman's reactions. They accept responsibility, but they want to know the consequences. They're not *wired* the same as men, they tend to plan better and consider the long range implications. On the other hand, men take risks, but they're often based on the immediate pay-off, without consideration of the longer range. Properly combined, these two approaches can benefit a company tremendously.

---

[1] Research performed in 1989 by Drs. Russell Clark and Elaine Hatfield as discussed in The Willingness to Respond, in the book "Love Cycles" by Winnifred B. Cutler, page 182, published 1991 by Villard Books.

Venusians, Martians, and Jerks

Rob Becker, in his broadway show *Defending the Cave Man*, delivers a parody of John Gray's *"Men Are From Mars, Women Are From Venus"*. It goes something like this:

Now, I'm going to explain something lots of you have been hearing about, and I call it Women are from Venus and Men Are Jerks. You see, you start with a group of men. They're sitting in the living room watching TV. One notices that the chip bowl is getting low, so he says, "Hey, the chips are getting low!" This passes the response to the next guy, who answers, "I filled the bowl the last time!" And the third guy says, "Yeah, and I carried them in from the car." And the fourth one completes the round: "I got out the bowl!" The last guy, realizing he has lost, stammers out, "Well, ahh, I helped, ahh, eat the chips?" and then slinks out to the kitchen to refill the bowl.

Now picture the same scene with a group of women. One of them notices that the chip bowl is getting low and says, "Hey the chips are getting low" and the second woman says "I'll take it out and fill it!" To which the third chimes in, "The dip is getting a little low too, so I'll come along." And the third woman joins in with, "I'll help mix up some new dip." The last woman, not wanting to be left behind, offers "I'll come and get some more cold drinks." And before you know it, there's a ladies conga line dancing into the kitchen.

And that's why, the comedian explains, women are from Venus, and Men Are Jerks.

Aligning the Planets

So how does this come into play in the workplace? Well, when handing out assignments, a good manager remembers that women are willing to take on responsibility. If you need them to cycle back to you before taking action, you need to be clear and direct about this.

Men, on the other hand, may be reluctant to push their responsibility. So if you need them to take over for you and finish the job without waiting for further instruction or approval, make sure they understand this as well.

```
----------------------- Message ------------------------
To: Laura Ricci
From: George Wilkerson
Subject: Politics

Laura-

Let's see if I have this right. I shouldn't have a problem with
women accepting responsibility, but I need to make sure they
don't accept TOO much. Whereas, with men, I need to make sure
they know WHEN they're resopnsible. Is that it?

----------------------- Message ------------------------
To: George Wilkerson
From: Laura Ricci
Subject: Who's Responsible for What?

Bingo
```

AS A RULE:

- **Remember that women take responsibility and men leave it.**
  Stay aware of the difference between the way men and women handle an assignment.

- **Make assignments of responsibility clear.**
  Don't rely on the *lines* of responsibility.

- **Want to know about "consequences?" Ask the women.**
  They're more accustomed to thinking of them.

EXERCISE BREAK

This exercise should give you a chance to prove for yourself the effects of gender identification. You'll need two children, a boy and a girl (preferably your own.) All you need to do is ask each of them the same question, one that's associated with a task: "Will you see about taking the dog out for a walk?" Or "Will you see about the trash in the kitchen?" Or "Will you see about the bed linens?" But ask each of them separately, out of earshot of the other. And make sure you phrase it that way. Don't ask them to perform the task.

THE BOY'S RESPONSE:

_____

_____

THE GIRL'S RESPONSE:

_____

_____

Did the girl complete the task simply at your suggestion and the boy assume the least portion of the task (looking to see if the dog has a collar on, reporting the level of the trashbag, or straightening the bed sheets rather than changing them.)?

The fact that children demonstrate these differences illustrates that this inclination begins early in life and is more likely to be a result of our biological wiring than learned behavior.

You may see some "grey area" in the responses. That's why we suggest you consider where someone fits on this scale when selecting techniques, not simply whether they produce testosterone. With a female who registers toward the male end of the scale, you may have success using some male approaches.

19

CHAPTER 3

When the Chain of Command Is a Web

Tim and Judy share an office; their relationship is friendly and sometimes they talk about outside matters, but for the most part, their conversation is work-related. That's how the subject of Tim's inability to get his computer system upgraded came up. "I've been here longer than a lot of other people who got upgrades," he complained. "It's almost as if they intentionally pass me over."

Judy was sympathetic. She didn't get the upgrades either, but had chalked it off to seniority. She had only been with the company for a little over a year. "Have you asked anyone about it?" she said.

Tim nodded. "I sent an e-mail to my Unit Manager and he forwarded it to the Operations Staff Manager, but that was the last I heard of it."

"How long ago was that?" Judy asked.

Tim snickered. "Three...maybe four months."

And that was the end of the conversation. But the next day, when she was dropping off some items at Accounts Receivable, she asked the receptionist who handled purchasing for Tim's division. "That would be Tom Mullins."

The next morning, she dropped by Tom Mullins office. "Just checking on a rumor," she told him. "I hear we're getting another spread sheet upgrade."

Mullins shook his head. "We don't even have the last one distributed," he said.

"What's the hang up?"

"They found a bug in version 2.0," he explained. "So they sent us a patch; version 2.01 actually, though they never called it that. So we had to go back and reinstall the ones we already had in. And those were only put on selected machines."

"By seniority?," she said.

Mullins furrowed his brow at her. "Who told you that?" he said. "It's by project. We get a list of the current projects that require spreadsheets and install on the systems of people on those projects."

"Oh," Judy said. "I see. And the list comes from...?"

"The Operations Staff Managers."

That afternoon she asked Tim if his Unit Manager knew he was using the spreadsheet program on his project. Tim said he thought so; he had requested the upgrade, hadn't he?

"But did you tell him it was for your project?" she asked.

*He searched back through the e-mails. No, he hadn't. So Judy
explained the situation to him.*

Grandmothers quilt in circles; each has her own piece to add, but
they work together as equals, chatting across the developing quilt as
they go. Grandfathers sit on the porch and whittle; each has his own
piece of wood; each is creating something different. The culture of our
genders reflects our method of operating. Men see their organization as
a hierarchy, with layers and boxes; they must work their way "up the
ladder." Women see the organization as a web of people. Some are their
subordinates, some are their superiors. The result is that women more
naturally think in terms of the network of assistance and resistance they
face in completing their work. This is a strength which women add to
the mix.

Flexibility is greatest for those who see themselves in the organization as part of a network. They don't see just one way up in the organization if they run into a problem. The idea that you can call only on
those within your line of control and influence is limiting. Women have
the edge in this situation.

Whereas men think it's tidier and more orderly to follow a set of
rules, women intuitively recognize the bottlenecks of that approach. Men
don't see any need to talk to anyone from another area, so they usually
don't. Or if they do, they communicate up, trying to find someone at a
level of influence over their area. While this maintains good control, it
takes time and routinely involves searching higher and higher to find the
level assistance necessary to achieve the objective.

Women have a better understanding of the patchwork quilt which
is their workplace. They see the interconnectedness of the whole organization. Because they think more divergently, they can spot the critical
pieces of the quilt that affect their needs. To women, the organization

isn't a series of building blocks; it's a collection of interconnected units and there's no limit to the avenues of communication available to any of those units.

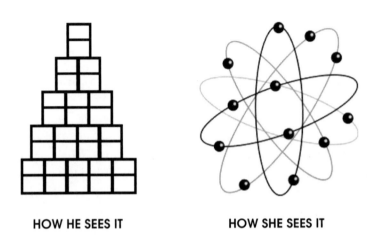

HOW HE SEES IT   **HOW SHE SEES IT**

If, For Instance...

...you're a mid-level manager who takes on a new client whose main office is in Beauregard, Alabama and you need a rush delivery, you check the list of approved shipping carriers for overnight deliveries. The only choice is Express Mail. They're one of the largest delivery services, and the contract you have with them provides handsome discounts for your company's business because you maintain high volumes of such rush deliveries. But Beauregard, Alabama is not served by Express Mail; the only one delivering there is *Determined Deliveries*, and they don't give discounts. So you double-check the company's policy and just to be sure, you ask Burt, in the shipping department, if Express Mail really *is* the required carrier for overnight delivery.

If You're a Man, You're Most Likely to...

...send a memo to *your* manager requesting help with this dilemma. He checks with the senior manager who takes it to the managers' group meeting, where they all agree that yes, Express Mail certainly is the exclusive carrier and they see no reason to change that. So you ask your boss to take the issue to the next level, his division manager. But the DM knows this isn't important enough to set aside other priorities, so finally looks at it later in the week and sends a note to the manager to explain that he can't do anything because shipping is handled by another department; however, he volunteers to take the issue to his own boss, who also supervises the head of Shipping and Receiving. The head of Shipping and Receiving recognizes that *Determined Deliveries* is the best solution, but he explains that a change in policy is needed. That's when the process of approving the change in policy begins. And after a couple of weeks, the customer's deliveries start.

Everything is orderly. No one's feathers got ruffled because their territory was intruded on by another department or division. Everyone in management is fully informed of the details necessary to deliver rush packages to the new client...a few weeks or months after the problem was discovered.

If You're a Woman, You're Most Likely to...

...talk to the mailroom clerk and explain the situation to her. She calls *Determined Delivery* and gets a current list of their drop off locations, confirms that they're the only ones delivering to Beauregard, Alabama, opens an account with them, and gets the first package out to them the same day. And if she's really on top of it, she gets a supply of their mailing labels.

Of course, if the organization is still tightly hierarchical, a number of bad things can happen. Whether a man or woman who takes the latter course of action, others in the organization might see it as thwarting protocol, breaking the rules, going behind someone's back, etc. When it comes time to re-negotiate the Express Mail contract, the new location may not be part of the deal if the manager in charge of the shipping department wasn't told about the problem. And even if the mailroom clerk passed it up to her department manager, it's up to the department manager to remember the incident; otherwise, nothing else will happen.

Furthermore, if the mailroom clerk is uncomfortable about doing things that don't follow the rules, she might go to her boss and complain. And yet...the female solution worked. It achieved the primary goal of any business, pleasing the client. It never became a problem for the client.

Shifting to a Unified Network Style

The way the organization functions is determined by the way it is described internally. In the traditional, male-dominated, hierarchical organization, the only available means for networking is to adopt a "skunkworks" mentality. Open communication is risky in a hierarchy, because the only orders one can legitimately follow are the formal operating procedures dictated from above. Those who circumvent the hierarchy are part of the "underground." They get things done, but at great risk to their careers. If our example happened in an organization with a true networked style, the woman's boss would explain to the mailroom guy that her solution is the only way to get the client what they want and if the mailroom guy wasn't responsive, she might even go to the mailroom manager and explain the situation.

Networked organizations seem chaotic, but they are responsive to the marketplace. Those in charge may fear chaos and rightfully so, since it's sure to lead to catastrophe if it gets out of hand. But, if open communication is the rule (perhaps the only rule), the workforce is empowered to take action. Then managers can begin describing themselves as part of a web, a network, where the value of the hierarchy diminishes. Sitting on the top is seen as the fringe, too far from the action to make rapid changes. Each group and member of each group sees the center of the circle as the heart of the organization. Rather than fearing being "stuck in the middle" they aspire to it. Positions "higher" in the organization are less effective because their occupants may be too far removed from the heart of the organization.

More than chaos, some managers in a newly networked organization feel a threat to their rank. It takes a special kind of leadership to administer this. In "The Prince and the Pauper," Mark Twain told the

```
--------------------------- Message ---------------------------
To: Laura Ricci
From: George Wilkerson
Subject: Shifting to a Network Style

This is all well and good in a perfect world, Laura, but what
do those of us inside the skunk works do if we want the
organization to move toward accepting the networked style? (I'm
referring to those without the clout to effect a change.)

--------------------------- Message ---------------------------
To: George Wilkerson
From: Laura Ricci
Subject: Shifting to a Network Style

The first step is exactly that... establishing a Skunk Works
mentality and working underground. The second step is to
identify potential defenders within the hierarchy. At some
point, some success will come out of the Skunk Works that would
not have happened if the hierarchy had been followed and that's
when the Skunks need to be protected.

After a few successes, even the most entrenched will admit that
the Skunk Works has some value. That's when they'll try to
indoctrinate you or co-opt you back into the hierarchy. You
might have a few defectors then, but if you persist you can
make them realize it was the change in approach that caused the
success.

Of course, some organizations never recognize the value of the
Skunk Works; others give it respectful distance because they
don't want to taint its success, and a few will hold it up as
an example for others to emulate.
```

tale of two identical boys who traded places—one the prince of the kingdom, the other a pauper—and what the Prince found out as he walked around, unfettered by the royal bureaucracy and spoke to his subjects. Managers can't disguise themselves, but they can promote management by walking around.[1] This is just one way successful managers keep an organization truly networked and maintain an open communication stream.

---

[1] Thomas J. Peters, *Liberation Management, (Necessary Disorganization for the Nanosecond Nineties),* Thomas J. Peters, A.A. Knopf, 1992

Fostering "Crossgender Communication"

Men and women communicate differently. Women tend to listen to the content. It's easy for them to establish and maintain rapport with others because they are "active listeners." By nature, they seek to understand the meaning. As a result, they are more likely to find ways to align with and support the direction of the speaker.

Men use the time others are speaking to think about what they can say the next time there's an opening. They may not absorb as much of the content, but simply pick up the initial portion and run with it. Women are less likely to provide a rapid response or a differing position because they are immersed in the content. This does not mean they don't understand or have their own opinions. It simply means they need more time to digest before readying a response.

```
------------------------- Message -------------------------
To: Laura Ricci
From: George Wilkerson
Subject: Listening so far

OK, Laura. I'm listening. So what do I do when I'm leading a
meeting of men and women to make sure they listen to each
other?

------------------------- Message -------------------------
To: George Wilkerson
From: Laura Ricci
Subject: Listening so far

One way to do this is to encourage "Active Listening." Get each
person to echo back the message of the previous speaker. This
way you clarify, for yourself and the group, the speaker's
intention. You give the group another opportunity to hear the
message. This takes the focus off of the individual speaker and
broadens the focus of the listeners to the larger group.

If some members of your group aren't willing to do this, you
(the group leader) can do it. Furthermore, you can also read
back the message in hierarchical language; that might make it
more easily digested by those who might stray from the content.
(This might explain how the phrase "cross-functional teams"
came into being; a leader translating a description of a web to
language understood by the hierarchical types.)
```

Men listen to communication methods. They skim over the content (get the gist) and begin preparing their response before the speaker has finished. Sometimes this results in men being accused of not listening. Men more often have a response ready because of this method. This listening can be described as strategic because it allows a ready response crafted during the delivery of the previous message. It gives them the opportunity for manipulation of the listeners in their response. But it can be hard to get everyone together if most are busy preparing responses rather than absorbing the full message. In her book on womens' leadership styles, *The Female Advantage*[2], Sally Helgesen describes the advantage of the networked organization from the woman's perspective: *"She has direct access to anyone within the organization without having to resort to channels, and thus avoids the attendant risks of dilution and distortion."* Adopting the network expands this advantage to all members of the organization, regardless of gender. Most men find it's easier to let go of the hierarchy and join the web. Only the insecure males in your organization will have a problem with it. There also may be a few women, who have bought into the hierarchy and are unwilling to let go.

As an organizational model, the network makes obvious the many different routes to any particular goal. There's rarely, if ever, just one alternative. Because there are lots of routes to success, more action can take place, and less responsibility will be forfeited with a "that's not my job." In the hierarchy, it's easy to forfeit responsibility for completion of the action. "I've passed the ball to my boss; now it's in *his* court." But less gets done when everything must be approved by the few who are higher up in the organization.

HTML: The Influence of a New Communication Model

For years, the *menu* was the structural standard for PC software. A *Main Menu* presented a half dozen choices, and each of those presented

---

[2]Helgesen, Sally *The Female Advantage: Women's Ways of Leadership*, Doubleday Dell, 1990

a menu which branched off to a half dozen more and so on for layer after layer—a nice, neat hierarchical structure. Then came HTML (hypertext mark-up language) which removed the need for linearity. (We can't help but wonder if it ever existed in the first place; most programmers are men.) In HTML, *hot links* make it possible for the user to jump around in a document, branching off in a web-like environment with no need to move up and down through the system. Every user defines his or her own path and that path can be different every time.

Businesses worldwide are setting up web sites on the Internet at the rate of more than 3,000 a week and every web site uses HTML to link the information as well as linking to other sites. Furthermore, those same businesses are rapidly adopting Internet Web Browser software (Netscape®, Mosaic®, MS-Internet Explorer®) to create Intranets. Each computer on their LAN (Local Area Network) is linked and now their internal documents, e-mail, and other functions are becoming part of a web. One of the most dramatic results of this new structure is a change in the way people communicate. This change supports the concept of a unified network, a web of employees. People are learning that you don't have to go up and down, from complex to simple, or top to bottom. You can go just about any way you like, anywhere in the organization you like. As a result, the new majority functions in a very new way.

AS A RULE:

• **Keep communication open.**

This means you need to help the men move toward acceptance of the network of assistance and resistance in which they work.

• **Give those "close to the action" the freedom to make critical decisions.**

They're on the front lines; they know the client.

- **Support the HTML style.**

  Encourage your people to link thoughts and ideas in non-linear fashion, *outside the box.*

- **Help the men listen.**

  Ask them to repeat what others have said.

- **Help the women to contribute.**

  Hold meetings without outcomes; meet today, explore the topic, and come back tomorrow with your thoughts and ideas.

EXERCISE BREAK

Want to see YOUR web?

Complete the charts on the next page as follows. List everyone you work with or through. Then, score each person on their *Strategic Importance* on a scale of 1-10. After that, score each person on their *Problematic Importance,* and then score each person for the amount of contact you have with them. The relative scores between people for each of these three traits is what's important, so score each column before going on to the next column.

Now type this list and scores into your spreadsheet software and ask for a scatter diagram with labels[3] or plot each person on the chart by hand. You may be surprised where some of your contacts land.

If you'd like to change the score, take a few months and concentrate on changing the amount of contact you have with each person. For instance, if you notice that someone is quite high in Strategic Importance and Problematic Importance but you spend very little time with them, you could be looking for more opportunities to be in contact with them. This is how you'll learn more about what they need and their vision for the future, while they learn your perspective. When you re-score, you'll find they move away from problematic importance.

You may also find that there are some people with whom you have more contact than might be worthwhile. Folks who are time-wasters would be in this category.

---

[3]For a spreadsheet template for Lotus, Excel or Quattro Pro, visit our home page at http://www.R- 3.com/bookwork.htm and download the files for free!

Strategic Importance (Career and company progress is dependent on this relationship)			
Problematic Importance (Level of effort required to keep workflow operating smoothly)			Amount of Contact
Name			

Place a dot for each person in the chart. Use the vertical axis for **Strategic Importance** (Career and company progress is dependent on this relationship) and the horizontal axis for **Problematic Importance** (Level of effort which is required to keep workflow operating smoothly). The **Amount of Contact** you have with each person can be used to change the place they land on your chart. Increase the amount of contact if you want to try to lower the problematic importance or impact the opinion of someone with high strategic importance.

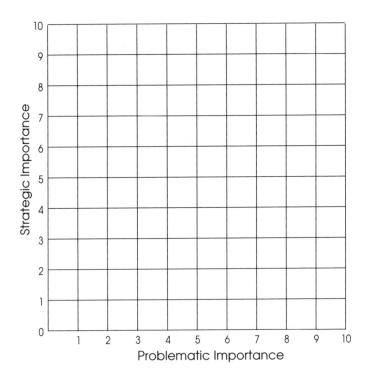

CHAPTER 4

Keeping Score and Scoring Points

The consultant presenting a training class was introducing some new sales concepts. Since he wasn't an employee, he wasn't familiar with many of the company's long-standing conventions and standard business practices, so no one was surprised when he contradicted a "corporate rule."

Todd, a new employee, questioned the consultant several times, clearly trying to resolve the contradiction between what the consultant was saying and what he had been told by his manager. "Are you sure that's the best way to do it?" he would ask. "I mean... I don't think that's the way it's done here." To which the consultant always replied. "Absolutely."

At a break, the Corporate Vice President who was sponsoring the training asked one of the managers about the questioning employee. "What's his problem?"

"He's a new guy," the manager said. "But maybe you need to make some kind of announcement; let the new people know it's OK to question things."

The V-P snickered. "I'm not going to do that," he said. "Let them figure it out for themselves."

The new employee figured it out quickly. He left a few months later. And nearly all of the women attending the training seminar also got the message. One by one over the next year each of them left the company."

Your employees **must** feel that they're getting the straight poop. Women are especially sensitive to the traditional, corporate metaphorical style of indirect communication. (We were told once that in order to succeed in the business world you had to understand people who spoke in parables.) The problem with the V-P's response to his manager is that it sent a message to the employees which was especially telling to the women: *You are not important enough to know the straight story."*

One Up and One Down

The golfers are returning to the clubhouse. The men are busy reliving their best shots, the holes where they shot par or under, their best drives, and they're dis'ing the duffers, making fun of their errors and lack of style. There's almost a second competition to see who can brag the most or dish out the worst insults.

The women are reviewing their score sheets and comparing their successes and failures, taking each hole and focusing on the areas where they need to improve, sharing criticisms and offering advice.

Because men and women, you see, keep score quite differently. Whether it stems from environmental or genetic differences doesn't matter. Men are taught to get "one up" on each other because each one believes he'll have his day in the sun one day, his turn at being in charge. Just like a tussling litter of puppies, men realize that even if they lose today, they could very well win tomorrow. They're given that sense of "my turn will come" from an early age.

Women are generally raised "one down." They're told to "suck up" their disappointments. *Don't argue, don't fight and be a nice little girl.* They know they won't ever be "king of the hill," so they keep careful

```
------------------------- Message -------------------------
To: Laura Ricci
From: George Wilkerson
Subject: New Age Little Girls

Laura: If there's one place where I think there has been a
change it's what women tell their daughters in this area. Most
of the women I know don't tell their daughters to "be a nice
little girl." These days, many more of them teach them to
"stand up for yourself; don't let them push you around." (Or am
I fantasizing again?)

------------------------- Message -------------------------
To: George Wilkerson
From: Laura Ricci
Subject:

I don't believe it. I see "new-age" parents who as managers
evaluate women on their ability to get along while evaluating
men on their ability to get something done. And I haven't yet
seen a parent recount with glee the rough and tumble of a fight
their daughter has instigated.

What I do see are parents trying to use the female model for
both male and female children. Be peaceful, stand up for
yourself but be nice about it, don't worry, you can go do
something else if they won't let you play.
```

track of points. Without an opportunity to struggle and win, women remember the score and they count every slight.

Too often, poor managers ignore women's complaints while promptly correcting those the men make. This reinforces the sense in women that they rank below the men, and their only alternative is to be quiet. But what those managers don't realize is that the women are quietly keeping score.

Instead, they see the women as picking on inconsequential things— and no wonder, since if they don't have a chance of being heard on matters of consequence, that's all there is left. But instead of talking to them, the manager simply wonders "Did we hire the wrong women?" rather than asking himself. "Did our management make them into 'wrong' employees?"

The Fee for Overdrafts Just Went Up

In *The Seven Habits of Highly Effective People,*[1] Stephen Covey explains relationships through the bank account metaphor. Those relationships with high positive balances build trust by keeping commitments, assuring honest relations, and sharing respect. Small withdrawals are no problem. But in those relationships where the *emotional bank account* is low, even slight withdrawals can move the account into overdrawn status.

Just as the relationship with your banker changes once you've overdrawn an account, the relationship between people requires enormous energy to repair once it is overdrawn. And that's doubly so with women. They keep a balance sheet. This is the place in which you can become "an offender for a word." When the account is overdrawn, every infraction is retained. (*"And there's something else you did in 1972 that wasn't so hot either!"*) With a consistently overdrawn bank account, the petty, small infractions take on greater significance.

---

[1] 1989, Fireside of Simon and Schuster. Page 188.

How Management Tilts the Scales Against Itself

If a male manager avoids building relationships with the women in the workforce and simply concentrates on building relationships with the men, the payoff is simple. The women get the message and keep track of those who impeded their progress. Avoid direct communication and open discussion with women and you invite recrimination. Women do not forget, and it's a mistake to expect them to.

In the skirmishes of traditional political infighting, which some organizations condone, the men have an advantage. Males aren't mortally wounded in the skirmishes, and many actually relish getting back into the game. They've developed "thick skins." Sensitivity is not valued. Working side by side with those who back-stabbed them yesterday is accommodated. As we mentioned earlier, most men expect they'll get their own day in the sun soon enough.

```
-------------------------- Message --------------------------
To: Laura Ricci
From: George Wilkerson
Subject: Overreacting

Laura: Don't you think some of the men who are brusque with
women have been scared by the sexual harassment thing? It may be
that their brusque behavior is a way of overcompensating, to
make it clear that they aren't making advances or doing anything
untoward. I know that I tend to do this especially if I find a
woman attractive.

-------------------------- Message --------------------------
To: George Wilkerson
From: Laura Ricci
Subject: Overreacting

I do too. I think we all realize that body language and
subconscious cues can send messages we have no intention of
acting on. That's why we overcompensate with a stricter
business-like behavior, to counteract the message we are afraid
might be going out.

Once sent though, I'm usually able to ease up later on and
establish a more comfortable relationship without mistaken
messages.
```

Generally, women are seriously upset by the skirmishes. They weren't really anxious to play the game in the first place, especially if they suspect they can't win. And why associate with or play with cheaters if you know you'll never win? Often, they create their own game, but more than likely they withdraw and go play someplace else (like, your competitor's organization.) But the men close ranks and jump back into the game. *"Guess she just couldn't take it,"* they say, or *"She wasn't what we needed anyway."* The danger is that, in the long term, the organization has lost a critical viewpoint.

Are YOU Keeping Score?

Look at attrition in your workplace by gender. If it's higher for women, it's a symptom of this problem. And if you want to do something about it, you'll need to make some changes in how you operate.

AS A RULE:

Avoid metaphorical communications.
Be direct and honest.

Don't ignore women's complaints.
Ask yourself what you would do if a man had come to you with the same issue.

Always clear the air.
Make sure that conflicts are resolved to everyone's satisfaction. It's not easy for a manager (regardless of gender) to be sure this is happening, but it's critical if you want to harness the benefits of diversity in your workforce.

EXERCISE BREAK

Check the files on the last few employee evaluations you did, thinking back to the discussion you had with the women.

- Did any of the women bring up *insignificant* issues?

  YES ___   NO ___

- If YES, could these have been trial balloons to see if it is safe to bring you larger issues?

  YES ___   NO ___

- What actions did you take as a result of these evaluations?

- Did you tend to take action more often on the men's or women's issues?

CHAPTER 5
He's a Shaker; She's a Mover

M*ary Trujillo began as a legal secretary and worked her way up to a position as an assistant manager in the Worker's Compensation division in a large law firm. During that time, by taking classes in the evenings, she had become certified as a paralegal, although the certification simply confirmed what everyone in the office already knew. Her experience had taught her more about workmen's comp law in her state than anything she could have learned in a certification program.*

Mark Simmons had also worked his way up and, recognizing Mary's skills, brought her along with him. Mary knew that over time she had become the lynchpin in Mark's operations. She also knew that Mark's drinking had become more of a problem over the last few years, but she had stayed by him.

This year, however, things were different. Mary was a single parent and her son was having emotional problems. She realized that she not only needed time to help him, but also needed more money to pay for the treatment program. She went to Mark and explained the situation. She told him that now that she had her paralegal certificate, she had moved to a higher level in her field. What she really wanted, she said, was a promotion, a recognition of her skills and contributions. What she didn't tell him was that covering for him on those occasions when he was drinking wasn't in his, or her, best interests.

She wasn't at all prepared for his reaction. "Your personal problems are your own Mary," he said. "And your professional status is no different now than it was when you signed on."

She was shocked, but she said nothing. She knew that her job opportunities had widened now that she had her certificate. And her reputation would support any kind of move she had to make. Within three months she had a new, higher paying job as the manager of the Workmen's Comp section of a bigger law firm.

Most of us work under a covenant, not a contract. Max DePree in *Leadership is an Art* said, "Three of the key elements in the art of working together are how to deal with change, how to deal with conflict, and how to reach our potential. A legal contract almost always breaks down under the inevitable duress of conflict and change. A contract has nothing to do with reaching our potential."[1] Having a contract with your employees is a legal requirement; what you need to create is a covenant.

As DePree explains it, the contract may provide the terms of employment, but the covenant gives meaning to the work and makes it

---

[1] Max DePree, *Leadership is an Art*, page 59, Dell Publishing. 1989

possible to create a relationship that can withstand conflict and change. Nonetheless, there are still managers who think that a contract takes care of every-thing (and they wonder why there's no loyalty to *The Company*), and some employees who think that if they have a contract they're *set for life* (and wonder why there's no loyalty to *them.*)

Moving on Up

A man improves his chances for success by standing with the "winners" in the organization or carving out a niche and racking up points. He can either "hitch his wagon to a star," or "play to win." A woman improves her chances of success by moving out and up. She can remain "stuck in Mobile with the Memphis blues" or "fly away home."

```
------------------------- Message -------------------------
To: Laura Ricci
From: George Wilkerson
Subject: Climbing Jacob Inc.'s Ladder

I think the whole contract for life thing is disappearing pretty
fast. The down-sizing trend of the last few years has put that
idea to rest for a lot of men AND women. So...what does a
company do? Do we assume that women knew all along not to depend
on the company career ladder, or do we try to "get back that
lovin' feeling?"

------------------------- Message -------------------------
To: George Wilkerson
From: Laura Ricci
Subject: Climbing Jacob Inc.'s Ladder

The "contract for life" was a boon for deadwood. And it was an
excuse to require folks to wait for the next promotion round
rather than look for opportunities elsewhere. In the long run,
organizations and people will be better off in a more fluid,
dynamic marketplace in which everyone is on "temporary loan"
because organizations won't stagnate and people won't find their
work unwelcome drudgery.

Most organizations can't provide the ideal situation to every
valuable employee, every year. The way to hold onto the valuable
employees is to make sure that they're getting the opportunities
that fulfill them. And that's much easier said than done.
```

But some women's efforts to advance are thwarted long before they reach levels of any significance. This is partly due to the "glass ceiling" phenomenon and partly because the males in the organization are not gender-blind. They simply can't conceive of any woman being in a position other than the one she logged into when she joined the firm. If she wants to be promoted as quickly as her male peers, a woman has to move to another organization.

What this means to organizations with a focus on long-term employment is that they have to find ways to assure that women are given as much of an opportunity to be promoted as men. And that has to be done in a way that doesn't threaten men. We saw an excellent example of the problems this creates with the Affirmative Action backlash. Rarely, if ever, was a qualified white male passed over for an unqualified minority male or female. And yet, the general feeling is that this was happening. And so there emerged the *angry white male* who was credited with the Republican election victory in '94.

While some managers argue that high turnover rates mean fresh blood, the more astute among them acknowledge that the high costs of training and orientation for new employees could be better spent on other activities. The U.S. Army knows well the value of the career soldier. The taxpayers money is not well spent on a draftee who spends 18 months of a two-year hitch learning how to march, clean a rifle, read a radarscope, and track a missile.

Shopping

A man knows what he needs and looks for it in one brief shopping trip. A woman, on the other hand, values shopping. If she can't get what she wants with one employer, she'll simply shop for a more fluid situation.

Managers must recognize contributions before the employee has achieved tenure. This is important, but more so for women than men. Men are willing to accept a bonus check or the feeling that they're part of "the gang." Women feel "stuck." And once they feel they've accomplished their objectives, if there's no recognition, they're ready to move on. They don't need the bonus check or membership in the gang to feel appreciated. But public recognition of their contribution by management, especially if it's communicated to their peers (regardless of gender) goes a long way.

Reading the Barometric Pressure

Retirement vesting is a good barometer of senior management's attitudes. Consider the consequences of joining an organization with creeping retirement benefits. The average tenure for women is less than 4.5 years. For men it's over six years. When a retirement plan vests toward the far end of seven years, who benefits? Organizations set the level at a point just beyond the turnover rate they want to influence, so those workers hang on a while longer to collect.

Another measure of the organization's barometer is the difference in the its response to men and women who are passed over for a promotion. Some men can overcome the slight and continue up the ladder easily. Some organizations make a conscious effort to re-establish trust with the man and reassure him that his future is bright. (This may come from some misplaced sense of guilt for having bruised the man's ego.) You'll rarely see the same thing happen with women. Once a woman's attempts to get a promotion are thwarted, the organization sets the limitation as a matter of unwritten policy and regards her situation as permanent. Many women, as a result, develop a sixth sense; it's not female intuition. It's just that most of us know when we're not wanted. Women passed over are often ignored or told that they shouldn't be impatient.

Is It Time to Go?
(But it's still early!)

There's a cliche in the movies and television where a couple is at party and the woman is trying to get the man to leave. Usually, he's had too much to drink, or there's another woman there who's flirting with him. The cliche works because there's some truth to it. Women seem to have a better sense of when it's time to leave.

Even though the woman may be right, when the man asks the host or hostess if they should leave, the answer is always the same. "Of course not...have another drink," or "the night is young!" At the party, that response is a matter of courtesy. But the same courtesy holds true at the office. Making someone feel that they're staying beyond their welcome may be the most stifling thing a manager can do. The employee's frame of mind deteriorates, future opportunities are obstructed. As we said, men are more often sent a different message. "You didn't get the promotion," they're told, "but stick around. Something will open up eventually." Women, though, wrestle just as hard in an organization, trying to make a difference, and then, when the promotion goes to someone else, they simmer until their rage drains them of any power they might have had .

And the women who "hang in there" sometimes stay too long. After a while, they may not be able to present their best face, and so miss the best opportunities. Eventually, the successful career woman learns to avoid this. They polish that sixth sense and know when it's time to go.

A Career Ladder Is Not a 12-step Program

The nature of women is to be nurturing. In personal relationships this can lead to an unhealthy kind of co-dependence if they're paired with the wrong man. On the job it can have disastrous consequences. The women with this co-dependent kind of loyalty stay too long. The organization may have stopped providing a win-win match for the woman's talent, but much like the "battered woman" she stays and, over time, she becomes angry and disillusioned, unloading her grief throughout the halls to anyone who will listen. The damage to the morale of others can be substantial. It's dangerous for the women and risky for the companies.

These women, who are too loyal for too long, do the most damage to themselves. They join the chorus of whiners you'll find in every organization. Their usefulness to the organization, as well as to themselves, diminishes, and when that's gone they cannot represent

```
-------------------------- Message --------------------------
To: Laura Ricci
From: George Wilkerson
Subject: The Whiners

Laura-
You touched a nerve with the whiners. I have to ask: don't you
think whining is associated with women more than men?

-------------------------- Message --------------------------
To: George Wilkerson
From: Laura Ricci
Subject: The Whiners

Absolutely. I see women all the time who become whiners because
they stayed too long in an organization that has them pigeon-
holed. After a few attempts at getting promoted, they stop
trying and begin whining about the situation. Unfortunately,
this happens to a lot of women with great promise. They just
don't see that they have been pigeon-holed and that the managers
can't imagine them higher up in the organization. It's when they
don't leave that they hurt themselves most.
```

themselves as the competent, strong, effective souls they once were. They have come to believe they are not capable anymore. They eventually seek help and that's when the lawyers come in and government regulators begin calling.

AS A RULE

Create a Covenant

Whether or not you have a contract with your employees, you need to create a covenant. A covenant is a mutual agreement which gives meaning to the work and makes it possible to create a relationship that can withstand conflict and change. A covenant changes as the parties add or subtract items by mutual agreement. No surprises.

Prevention Is the Best Cure, But...

If you've let a situation with an employee go too far, the fresh air of a new perspective may be the only solution. Both for the employee and the organization. Generosity then becomes your only defense. Help them find their way out of the organization.

EXERCISE BREAK

Take out your calendar and answer the following questions by reviewing your social engagements.

- How many social functions did you go to with men from your organization over the last six weeks?

  _____

- How many social functions did you go to with women from your organization over the same period?

  _____

Now review your meetings with clients.

- How many meetings with clients did you decide to invite a man from your organization?

  _____

- How many did you invite a woman to?

  _____

Inclusion is the first step in changing the message to women that they are not important enough to be the future of your organization.

- Do you need to make plans to include women (or men) more often?

CHAPTER 6

How the Nest Was Won

J ason was a very popular employee in a very intense industry. The market was product driven and the need to develop upgrades and improvements was continual. No sooner would one product ship than the next version was being tested and readied for market.

At first, Jason liked the pressure. He enjoyed the long hours and hanging out at the office on the weekends. In some ways, he had found the family he never had when he was growing up. (His father had always been at work, even on holidays.) He was appreciated and consistently received good reviews and high praise, as well as bonus checks when a new product made it out in time to beat the competition.

When he met Ann, he didn't really want to get involved. But we all know how that goes... year later they were married, a year after that they bought a house and were planning a family.

Jason started looking around for another job, one with less pressure and more flexibility. And given his talent and proven skill, it wasn't long before he found one. The salary and benefits were the same, but the company was in a mature market, and needing less onerous dedication. So when the job was "in the bag" he turned in his notice.

The next day he received a call from the Vice-President. "Roger tells me you're a good man," he said. (Roger was Jason's immediate supervisor.) "He doesn't want to lose you."

Jason smiled. "I appreciate that."

"So how much do you want?"

Jason was taken back. "Pardon?"

"How much? We don't usually do raises at mid-year, but if that's what it takes..." Jason shook his head. "It's not about money," he said. "It's about time. I'd work for the same salary if I knew I'd have most weekends free."

The V-P snickered. "I can't promise that," he said. "I know," Jason replied. "That's why I'm leaving." The V-P shook his head. "We've got deadlines..." he began.

Jason extended his hand. "And I've got a life now," he said, smiling. "Thanks for your time."

The Days of the DINKS

During the 1940's and 50's, workers were taught to *leave your personal problems at home.* Once you came to the workplace, your heart and soul belonged to the company. Well, that philosophy doesn't cut it today. Very few workers these days have a housewife at home who insulates them from the pressures of home life. Even office wives (those doting secretaries who picked up your dry-cleaning and made sure the coffeepot was filled) have been downsized out of the company. And the ones who remain will usually tell you "That's not in the job description."

The risk of being fired is only half the threat it was for the last generation. The maturation of the baby boomers and the DINKS (double-income, no kids) has produced a workforce that's more volatile and mobile than any in history. Even though most families are dependent on two incomes, one employer rarely controls the family's entire income. As a result, men and women both have greater freedom to jettison a job. Holding the attention and dedication of the workforce is more difficult than was in the last generation.

```
----------------------- Message -------------------------
To: Laura Ricci
From: George Wilkerson
Subject: Another Lingering Image

Laura-

I didn't always have an absentee Dad, I have another image of my
father. He got laid off once and after about a week of having
him around I couldn't wait to get rid of him. (I think my Mom
felt the same way.) The fact was that he didn't know what to do
with himself. Are you saying that the men of today are different
in that respect?

----------------------- Message -------------------------
To: George Wilkerson
From: Laura Ricci
Subject: Another Lingering Image

Of course you are. And so are the women. Most of us remember
the unbalanced lifestyle of our parent's generation, and are
trying to find a better balance among the elements we value in
our lives.

Work that is valuable to the employee will still have a high
priority, but we are all seeking a better balance so that we
know our children before they are grown, and have developed our
own presence in the world rather than just our employer's.
```

A New Kind of Balancing Act

Although women have entered the workforce in greater numbers, they never lost the focus on home and children. Despite the Women's Movement and its *liberation*, the majority of women retain their orientation toward the family. In fact, the net result of these efforts seems to have had more impact on men. At the same time as women entered the workforce, men's goals and aspirations started to change. They began to realize that they did not want to die saying, "If only I'd spent less time at the office." They were raised in families where father was more of a paycheck than a recognizable face, and they feel that's a mistake they don't want to repeat.

Today we have a new kind of workforce. People want a "balanced lifestyle." They don't see their career as their life. Their hearts and souls belong to them, not to the organization.

Team Time-Outs

Have you noticed how easy it is to spot the best teams in an organization? What do they share? Well, they're usually dedicated to a goal, they're energetic about getting there, and they believe that they can make a difference. But if you talk to the managers of these teams, you'll find that there's something else going on: *time off.* And they guard it with a vengeance. The team members and the managers understand how important it is to be able to regenerate the batteries.

An army may run on its stomach, but a workforce runs on its time off. If you don't recognize that most of your employees are half of a family unit and that either one can easily seek employment elsewhere, you won't notice your turnover rate rising. Company loyalty based on simply having a job, is a thing of the past. If there's a job that gives more time and flexibility, they'll find it.

Because each worker is only one half of the family cash flow, they have more flexibility to leave and greater flexibility in negotiating the terms of employment than ever before. In *The Dilbert Principle*[1] Scott

---

[1] *The Dilbert Principle: A Cubicle's Eye View of Bosses, Meetings, Management Fads, & Other Workplace Afflictions*, by Scott Adams, Harper, June 1, 1996.

------------------------- Message -------------------------

To: Laura Ricci
From: George Wilkerson
Subject: Getting the job done

You're gonna love this, Laura. Sexist as it may sound, I think
that women are much better managers of their time than men. And
I think it's due to their history of staying home and having to
take care of things without supervision. Most of the women I've
had as managers had no problem with my time being flexible.
They were much better at focusing on whether or not I was
getting the job done.

------------------------- Message -------------------------
To: George Wilkerson
From: Laura Ricci
Subject: Getting the job done

I agree. Women are accustomed to juggling and whether it's
innate or they have developed a better sense of organization, I
certainly see more of this capability in women. And I wonder
sometimes if men like to have their workforce underfoot as a
territorial sort of trophy. I remember a male manager walking
into my area and asking where two of my staff were. I said I
didn't know, and he scoffed as if that meant I was a poor
manager because I didn't track everyone's whereabouts each day.
His group were retired in place, while mine was beating the
competition with a huge club. I doubt he's made the connection
yet.

Someone complained to me that my secretary had taken a day off
to attend a "kindergarten graduation" and they were annoyed
that she had "taken a day off just to do that when we needed
her here at the office." I don't care that one employee is
taking their time off to climb Mount Everest, and another is
taking their time off to break in a new puppy. They both get
their time off guarded, because that's their right — they
earned it. I now ask the people on my team to simply say they
will be out of the office rather than elaborate as to their
whereabouts. This seems so simple, I don't understand why
ANYONE would take the chance of sabotaging their team's
dedication by ever doing any differently!

Adams describes a management model in which managers plan to have
everyone *Out At Five.* The company isn't willing to settle for lower
productivity, just less time. Since a company can do much to kill
creativity, the trick is to stay out of the way of the workers and let them

find their own best ways to charge the batteries. Anderson Consulting may be using this concept in their program of *7 to 7* travel policy. Their consultants are asked to schedule their travel so that no one leaves home before 7:00 a.m. on Monday and arrives back home no later than 7:00 p.m. on Fridays.

Dilbert is not the American adult's most popular comic strip for nothing. Scott Adams has struck a note with workers, and that note resonates with most of us. Managers who want to inspire their teams need to thoroughly understand what is so hypnotic about Dilbert's message. The resonating note is that the balanced approach is the best way to get the best from each person. And the only way to do that is to focus more on their best and less on squeezing out every drop of their energy. As long as you have the best talent of an outstanding salesperson, do you really need to force them to become an accountant and fill out tedious forms and spreadsheets?

If you have a creative soul, and that talent helps you, don't you see a need to pay homage to the creative spirit and allow a few peculiarities? Even when they come into your office to announce that they have put a curse on a co-worker and that it seems to be working?[2]

Every game needs a referee willing to call a time out. It's one of those "Healthy Rewards," and it's universally recognized and appreciated. Your workers will be more likely to produce quality work if they know they're going to get quality time off. And quality, remember, is in the eye of the beholder; it's different for each employee. The more flexibility you can provide, the more loyalty you'll get.

---

[2] From Love & Profit, The Art of Caring Leadership by James A. Autry, William Morrow & Co. 1991.

AS A RULE:

Negotiate time off
When people are given more control over their time, most will use it more productively.

Call for a *Time Out.*
The only way to get the best from each person is to focus on their best effort, not how much time they spend.

Relish difference.
Don't be reluctant to provide some recognition to the person who isn't exactly a mainstream employee.

EXERCISE BREAK

Pop Quiz! Answer these questions as honestly as you can:

- What is the silliest thing an employee of yours has taken vacation time to do? (You DID give them the time off, didn't you?)

_____

- What is the most important thing an employee of yours has taken time off to do?

_____

- What can you do to make sure your environment protects everyone's right to use their time off as they see fit?

_____

- Did you tell anyone at work the silliest thing you've taken time off to do? (You HAVE taken time off to do something unusual, haven't you? If not, figure out what you should do that you've never thought was important enough, and schedule time to do it!)

_____

_____

CHAPTER 7

Good Relations Make
Good Vibrations

Belinda was in charge of a newspaper section. In addition to overseeing the production of the document, she had to coordinate the activities of the contributors, and then get the grids to production by deadline. She put the section to bed and went home. But in her absence, a glitch occurred on the production floor. Originally planned as a four-color spread, the shop called to say that their developer had "crashed" mid-way through the job. Belinda's staff couldn't reach her, so the shop contacted Belinda's supervisor.

He hesitated but they explained that the deadline was pressing. They could try to find another print shop and get it to them in the *hope that the job could be set up and redone in time, but that was iffy. Or they could print in a single color. The result wouldn't be as "pretty" but it would work all right. The supervisor paused for a moment and then told the shopmaster to go ahead and print single color.*

When Belinda came in the next day, the first person she saw was her supervisor. He didn't pull rank and he didn't act condescending. "I had to change the cover while you were out," he said. "I hope it's all right." He expressed respect for her original decision and he made sure that her authority was never questioned. What he provided was a model for Belinda's group and, in the process, assured Belinda their respect as well.

Belinda's manager was respected by everyone because **he** respected **them**. They knew he respected them because he was honest with them and deferred to their expertise. He was secure enough to recognize that when they did well he did well too. On those occasions when he was forced to intervene, he did it reluctantly, and was always very plain about it.

Me? A Nazi?

Most managers know that fear and intimidation breed hostility and anxiety. They rarely admit that they use such tactics, but of course, they're thinking of the extreme forms, the "Nazi" behavior of a fascist leader, not the more subtle forms employed by many corporate managers. What they can't see are the results of fear and intimidation: the reduction in the willingness of their employees to make suggestions and share new ideas. The formula is so simple that you wonder why they don't understand it—the relationship between the likelihood of being embarrassed and the willingness to speak out is one to one. A shame-based management style always bludgeons creative suggestions or innovation.

For example, a manager who felt that participating in "Dress Down Friday" was much too improper just couldn't understand why his employees thought that he didn't respect them. He was one of the "lucky" ones who actually found this out when he was involved in a team building exercise with his group. *His* supervisor was wise enough to recognize that there were problems and suggest the exercise as a way to help him improve.

He Rules or
She Rules

The rules women play by are different than those that men follow. Men work from the basis of loyalty to one's superiors *regardless of what they do to them*, while women are only loyal so long as they are treated right.

Men have been taught that their turn to be "superiors" will come; they know they will be empowered. If they lose some skirmishes, they can roll over and play dead; they console themselves with the knowledge that someday they will be on top.

Women, on the other hand, are taught that they will be submissive most of their lives. They are raised without any expectation that they will ever get a turn as King of the hill. They are taught that their fate is to submit to the will of others, that this is "good." Since there is no later turn for them, when they lose skirmishes, there is no consoling them, their self esteem is marred. Their only defense is to lie in wait. An honest opportunity is not expected to allow them to redeem their self-worth, so many women hoard the hurts.

The downfall of a manager who is abusive or unethical is more likely to be designed, orchestrated or executed by a woman. A big raise or promotion will not buy back their loyalty. But one apology will wipe the slate clean. The big raise or promotion is more likely to sway a man. And he'll be more willing to engage again, even if the wrong is never rectified.

Women and men were both outraged when Anita Hill showed up to accuse Clarence Thomas, the man from whom she had accepted career favors. But the outrage of the men was quite different than that of the women. It came, in fact, from opposite ends of the spectrum.

```
------------------------- Message -------------------------
To: Laura Ricci
From: George Wilkerson
Subject: Who's On Top?

Laura-

You say men are taught they will be on top someday and women are
taught that they will be submissive. If they're taught, the
teaching can be changed. So, should managers work on changing
these things? Maybe we should shoot for a gender-free approach,
with something like unisex rules.

           ------------ Message ------------
To: George Wilkerson
From:  Laura Ricci
Subject: Who's On Top?

George-

This is a test right? Managers today must deal with people in
the workplace AS WE FIND THEM. It would be great to have some of
these issues mellow over the next few years because a gender-
free approach was taken in the next generation's upbringing.

However, much of what we are talking about is probably hard-
wired into each of us, and gender-free training will soften but
not eliminate the difference between men and women.

It is finally safe to admit what every parent of a girl and a
boy knows — male and female children are different. Somewhere
deep in our psyche, there are differences that may be important
to our future as a species, may guide us to better accomplish
the roles we will serve as caretakers of the next generation, or
may have some other as yet little understood purpose.

The only thing we can say for sure, is that men and women are
different and as managers we can build these differences into a
stronger team in the workplace.
```

Women did not feel that Anita Hill owed any loyalty to Clarence Thomas. They felt that she had every right to air her complaints, even though Thomas had helped her in her career. Men on the other hand, felt that Anita Hill didn't play by the rules. They felt that she should have either submitted official complaints and blown her career *at the time of the incident,* or she should have moved on and forgotten the whole thing. Most men especially felt she had no right to use Thomas for career help and then bring out complaints later.

But women feel that not only did Anita Hill have no choice at the time of the incident, she had no choice at the time of the hearings. She could not risk ruining her career by filing a complaint at the time the incident(s) occurred. Any complaint at that time would have injured her more than Clarence Thomas, and she and her family had struggled too long to get her where she was to throw it away on a system certain to ruin the victim. Years later, keeping silent about the incidents at the time of the hearings was, quite simply, unethical. Anita Hill had no big decisions, no realistic choices, she just did what she had to do.

The irony of the Hill-Thomas matter is that there's really no right or wrong, just a difference in viewpoints. Women make better team members because they can see those viewpoints. And their cooperative nature provides a model for team-building. A female manager once explained, "My boss makes me fight for every inch. I just want to talk it over, agree, and then move on to action."

The male-fighter approach can be very valuable when it's directed at the competition. The female-cooperation approach is valuable when it's directed at teams. Women have an easier time finding common ground and incorporating the best ideas from the group. Once the "game plan" is established, men tend to do better at carrying it into battle.

The point is that women not only tell the good about people they respect, which men do as well, but they also provide a more balanced picture of their detractors and enemies. Men tend to slant their descriptions to stay in line with their own loyalties. The picture of reality they provide is more distorted. Which perspective do you want?

The View from the Top

In a recent survey, *Catalyst*, a New York based research organization, asked 325 male corporate executive officers why more women were not at the top of their organizations. 82 percent cited "Lack of significant general management or line experience" and 64 percent said the women "weren't in the pipeline long enough." Furthermore, 49 percent of the male CEOs felt that women's progress in the last five years was greatly improved.

When Catalyst surveyed female executives, only 47 percent cited "lack of significant general management or line experience." But 52 percent cited "male stereotyping and preconceptions about women." And 49 percent of the men (but only 23 percent of the women) executives said "exclusion from informal networks of communication" was another cause.

Sheila Wellington, the president of Catalyst, explains the difference in viewpoint this way: "The women talk about what they've seen, heard and felt going up the corporate ladder...and the fact that they have to consistently exceed performance expectations in order to advance. These barriers aren't part of the male CEOs' experience, so naturally they don't talk about them."

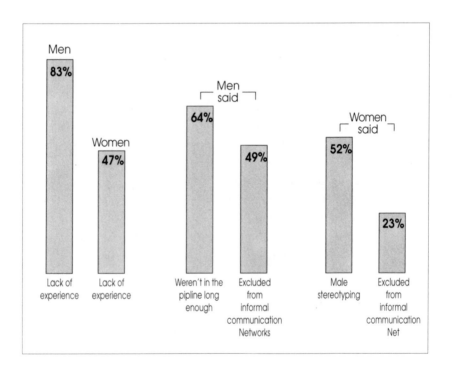

Part of the difference is the perspective of the players. Rarely do the privileged consider the trappings of the underprivileged to be an impediment to to the underprivileged rising from those ranks. The other difference is the gender orientation of the players. When men cited the reason for women being held back as "Not in the pipeline long enough" and "excluded from the informal networks of communication" they were certifying the "Old Boy Network" as alive and well. The women called the result "male stereotyping." Aren't both sides describing different sides of the same coin?

AS A RULE:

- **Don't Just Let 'Em Eat Cake**
  Eat cake with them when they celebrate.

- **Don't isolate yourself from those who work for you.**
  And don't ever think that you can't participate in an activity because it's "beneath" you.

- **Be loyal to your people**
  And they will be loyal to you. Remember that women will hoard their hurts. Treat ALL of the people who work for you with respect.

- **Get the picture from the women.**
  They're more likely to give a more complete picture of events and the personalities involved.

- **If you must fight, fight with the men.**
  They're more enthusiastic about winning. Women prefer to "help" rather than "fight to win."

EXERCISE BREAK

This exercise creates a window of your known and unknown traits. To do this, you need to get the help of at least 3 co-workers or associates who know you in the workplace. Give each a copy of the questions shown on the next page. They are asked to submit a list of descriptive words (i.e., bossy, dismissive, sensitive, good-listener, etc.). Make sure they are secure in the knowledge that their answers will remain anonymous.

While they're doing that, you should answer the same questions about yourself and fill out the table below with *your* responses.

When you get their responses back, add descriptions that are the same to the first column (along with your own). Circle words that are identical from your list or appear on more than one of theirs. Put all words that **don't** match yours in the boxes on the second column.

Postive traits I see:	Positive Traits I don't see:
Negative traits I see:	Negative traits I don't see:

To My Coworker:

I am interested in improving my management skills. Please help me by responding to the following questions. Be candid. Your responses will be combined with all the responses offered. The source of any comment is not important. The important thing is to gather candid descriptions. Your response will remain anonymous.

Be sure to use descriptive words (i.e., bossy, dismissive, sensitive, good-listener, etc.)

What do you see as my strengths?

_____

_____

_____

What do you see as my weaknesses?

_____

_____

_____

CHAPTER 8

Heroes and Heroines

D oris worked with Ted for nearly ten years. As Director, Ted took care of her, seeing to it that she was insulated from the higher ups who didn't understand her work. Over the years she had come to trust him. He would take the time to listen as she confided in him the details of her personal life.

Doris was nervous when she learned that the company was downsizing. Layoffs were planned, but Ted assured her that she was not on the "cut" list. And the first time, she wasn't. The department shrunk 35%, her work load increased, but she told herself "At least I have a job." During the next round of cuts, two more people in the department were laid off.

One day, Doris went to him with a problem. "I know there's another round of layoffs due. It's supposed to be the last one, but

I'm worried. I'm considering buying a house and..." Ted was nearly ecstatic. "What a wonderful idea. You've been wanting to do that for a long time, haven't you?"

Doris explained that yes, she had, but this round of cuts was coming and what if she lost her job and... "Not to worry," Ted told her. "Buy the house. You deserve it. I know it will make you very happy."

So she did. And one week later Ted called her in. "I'm sorry, Doris. They're closing our department," he said. "But I just bought a house." Ted nodded. "I know," he said.

"How am I going to make the payments?" she asked. "I'm sure you'll find another job," he said. "You're very good, very talented."

As she reached the door she stopped and turned to him. "Did you know this? Last week? When I asked you?" He nodded. "I knew how badly you wanted that house...." Doris was dumbstruck.

It was three months before she found another job. Doris was interviewed for both the Director and staff position in a new division. She was passed over for the position of Director and accepted the staff level position. "You almost had the Director's position," one of the senior managers told her one day, "but your former boss...Ted? When we spoke to him he told us that he didn't think you were ready for a management position. But he said you're an excellent team player and he thought you'd be ideal in the staff position."

Some men have difficulty dealing with women when the women become managers. A lot of men are raised with an image of an "ideal woman" who is virtually helpless so that the man can be her hero. And they stubbornly insist that every woman in the workplace (as well as those in their personal lives) must play that role. When that helpless female makes a move on her own, one which doesn't rely on the hero's help, she's seen as stepping outside the prescribed role. The reaction can be pretty dramatic, ranging from mild confusion all the way to extreme anger.

Living with A Time Bomb

The classic scenario is that of the male executive and the "office wife." It's the hero and the victim game and it's easy for the participants because they each know their roles and they can handle anything that comes along. The team works well together, efficiently protecting and supporting each other. He's the mighty hunter; she's the dutiful mate, making sure his needs are supported so that he can take care of the big stuff.

A manager who has a pair like this working for him or her may have a time bomb waiting to explode. Usually, you can't separate the hero and the victim without starting a battle. Sometimes, you can break the spell by promoting the victim, placing her in new surroundings, but you'd better be ready to spend a lot of time treating the wounded, because the myth dies hard. When the former victim succeeds, you may hear the hero discounting her/his work or background. You've removed the victim and thus disrupted the game. Temporary assignments are one way to place the victim in new surroundings.

Because women are more likely to be in assistant roles, promoting the hero usually means that the victim follows him and the battle expands to include more players. The victim and the hero both become advocates of the myth and teach others to join in the game.

It's an Equal Opportunity Dilemma

Both men and women are tempted by the opportunity to be a hero or heroine. It's a very flattering role...when it works. The man isn't always on top in this scenario. Some women managers become heros for the men and women employees under them. You've probably seen them, the "maternal" manager who always comes to the defense of the underlings in her group. And she does it with a vengeance. (Don't go near that bird's nest while Momma's sitting on the eggs; you're liable to get your finger snipped off.) Assertive women often develop by watching THEIR hero and modeling their methods of battle. Sometimes these heroines are aware of their modeling, and they'll become role models for the women around them.

So, What's the Problem?

This mythological scenario is dangerous because there is always a third party to the myth: the persecutor. A persecutor gives the hero a reason to avenge, and the victim a reason to seek protection. If a competitor is the persecutor, you have a pretty powerful force driving performance. Too often, though, the persecutor is more immediate, someone or some group within the organization, the entire organization, or even worse, your clients. In this way, the persecutor role eventually becomes destructive to the organization. That's why you must watch for this mythical battle and be willing to intercede.

For male heroes, the persecutor is often his peers. For female heroes, it's often her superiors. And more often than not, when the victim has learned her lessons well and gets the promotion, the former hero turns on her. To paraphrase Shakespeare, Hell hath no fury like the hero whose victim abandons her role. The victim, by imitating the hero in assertiveness and action, (regardless of whether she realizes she's doing it or not) makes the hero feel unnecessary. The hero may be out of the new game, but as we've said before, he won't be out for long.

And, if the changes you initiate make the victim appear successful, you may hear the hero in the background discounting his or her work. Or worse, you may not hear it at all, even though it's happening.

Handing Out the Rewards

So you're a manager who is standing by and watching all of this. What to do? The answer lies with what we call *Healthy Rewards* and *Unhealthy Rewards*. Healthy Rewards are those benefits which result when an energetic team plays these roles against the competition. Performance is increased and the participants get raises, bonuses, and promotions. Healthy rewards are positive and motivating and tend to level the politics because they focus on substance rather than on "What who thinks about whom." When positive "lessons learned" are applauded and encouraged, the manager's applause and encouragement is a healthy reward. Discouraging gossip by refusing to engage in it or act on it is a healthy reward. (We'll talk more about what are healthy" rewards for men and women in the next chapter.)

Unhealthy Rewards are the things that under-mine the victims: cutting remarks, sabotaging promotions, and any other tactics which might

```
---------------------- Message -------------------------
To: Laura Ricci
From: George Wilkerson
Subject: Riding into the sunset

Laura
Do you really think any of this can be changed? When you
consider the models we see in films and on TV and the very
nature of men and women, it seems like your asking us to fight
our hormones.

---------------------- Message -------------------------
To: George Wilkerson
From: Laura Ricci
Subject: Riding into the sunset

So long as the roles don't get out of hand, and the persecutor
is appropriate, there is no reason to intervene. In fact, when
the persecutor is a threat to the whole organization (such as
the competition) then this is a very powerful way to do battle.

When these kinds of roles get out of hand, someone will need to
intercede or risk the organization.

When the persecutor is an internal entity, person or group, you
may not be able to stay competitive with too much energy being
spent on this internal battle. At this point, management should
become aware of what is happening so you have a way of
separating the players and taking action.

When the hero or heroine takes aim at a former victim, the
organization is risking losing the former victim at minimum. The
greater threat is also losing a lawsuit for discrimination—with
the vicitm providing lots of examples of how your hero or
heroine does battle.
```

be used to preserve the hero's mythical role. You hear a lot about them in discrimination suits. If management has chosen to stay out of the game, this is where it becomes threatening to the organization. Sometimes the victim dishes out unhealthy rewards to prevent her position being disturbed, but more often, the hero fights vigorously to preserve the status quo.

```
------------------------ Message -------------------------
To: George Wilkerson
From: Laura Ricci
Subject: How about a poem?

Hero's Work

"What's good in our work?" He asked the group.
When someone volunteered the benefit of one woman,
a chorus echoed "the leadership of the woman."
The man with the pen did not move to add her name to the board.
Her name is insignificant,
the chorus is insignificant,
the echo is Wrong and not what the Hero wants to hear.
"What else is good?" He continued.

------------------------ Message -------------------------
To: Laura Ricci
From: George Wilkerson
Subject: Hero's Work

Woah! I don't quite understand what you're saying here.
Besides, I thought I was the one who started the e-mails. Is
this a girl thing?

------------------------ Message -------------------------
To: George Wilkerson
From: Laura Ricci
Subject: Hero's Work

Maybe. If this is too obtuse, we can take it out, but it's
perfectly clear to me. I'm quite attached to it, so....

------------------------ Message -------------------------
To: Laura Ricci
From: George Wilkerson
Subject: Hero's Work

I'm getting a headache.
```

AS A RULE:

- **Separate the hero and the victim.**
  If you can't do that without starting a battle, see if you can't do something to place the victim in new surroundings.

- **Encourage "healthy" rewards.**
  And discourage gossip.

- **Stay ready to spend time treating the wounded.**
  Keep in mind that more information is exchanged during the office chat around the coffee bar than during any formal meeting.

EXERCISE BREAK

For this exercise you'll need to complete the following form.

Identify a Hero/Victim situation.

Who is the hero: _____

Who is the victim: _____

Who is their common persecutor? _____

(If you don't know who the persecutor is, you may need to investigate this to see who or what is the persecutor for this team.)

Are you spending a lot of your time treating the wounded?

Do you need to intervene?

Is the prosecutor an inappropriate "enemy"?

Is the victim being held captive by the herd?

You may hear the hero discounting the victim's work or background. Or worse, you may not hear it at all, even though it's happening.
Remember that more information is exchanged during the office chat around the coffee bar than during any formal meetings.

CHAPTER 9
Rewards and Awards

The day after Joan was passed over for a promotion she knew she was entitled to, she went to Bill's office and told him she was resigning. "I've accepted a position with another firm," she said. "They've been after me for a long time."

Bill was stunned. "But you know we've got big plans for you," he said. " We're going to do great things for you; you've got a future here. How can you be like this; you're walking out on us just when we need you the most."

Joan had been passed over twice for promotion. The last time it happened, they promoted someone SHE had trained. Despite the fact that she was a dedicated employee, her performance had always been met with lukewarm support and interest. This week she discovered that she had been left out of a training course to *which everyone else at her level was invited. The competition called and Joan took the call.*

Later that day, Bill was talking to his manager. "I guess she just didn't have what it takes after all." he said. "I don't know what her gripe was all about. It came out of the blue. Surely she realized that if we didn't promote the guys we promoted, they would have left."

"I know," his manager said. "I never thought Joan would leave.

Bill nodded in agreement. "The only reason I left her out of that last training course was because she knew the material backwards and forwards. Why spend the time to involve her?"

His manager agreed. "She could have made a valuable contribution," he said. "Let's not make a big deal about it. Don't wanna rock the boat."

When you're concerned about managing effectively, making certain that your pay schedule is fair to both men and women is just the beginning. There are studies galore showing that most people are not motivated by money. Regardless of what your employees might say during their annual review, the satisfaction of a good raise is short-lived. For most workers, it simply recognizes that their contribution is valued by the organization. It's satisfying in the immediate weeks following the raise, but it fades quickly.

Everyone, regardless of gender, wants more from the job than simply a good pay check. And what they want varies. Men and women are looking for different things, so even though the pay structure may be the same, the most effective methods for rewarding performance and impacting motivation can and should be different.

Win-Win? Not if You're Male!

Men want to be recognized as winners. They enjoy wrestling with their peers, struggling to become *King of the Hill*. And they don't mind at all if that means that someone else lost. You can't have a winner if you don't have a loser. So the *award for excellence* works well. In fact, any kind of comparative result is good, just so long as the others perceive it as a fair fight. They should be seen as having won over other individuals, or that their team won over other teams. Winning, for men, lets them take the role of the valiant tribal leader who returns from the hunt with a load of trophies (a string of fish, a couple of deer across the hood, etc.).

As we said earlier, women are better team players, so they place greater value on the success of "the body politic" rather than the candidate. Individual recognition doesn't mean as much to them. Their rewards need to be less trophy-like. For a woman, things like increased access and communication are high rewards.

Talking First or Asking Questions Later

Women talk first. They look for information before they take any action. One sure way to sabotage a woman's growth and development is to "let her to figure it out for herself." Women don't particularly like experimenting in a void; they're not into learning by failure. And they are more likely to seek information first from others. If they feel comfortable coming to you, you have the opportunity to be a mentor and helper. If they don't feel welcome by their manager, they seek out another communication source. But if they go to those in your workforce who are disgruntled and willing to listen in return for the opportunity to add their complaints, the information they get is likely to be counter-productive.

Men actually use action as a way of generating information. While mentors can be helpful for men, exploring and experimenting on their own is usually more invigorating. The mentor to a man is usually welcome once some discovery has taken place. The mentor provides guidance for further investigation or acts as a sounding board to confirm that the investigation was done well.

You Can't Have Your Company Cake
and Eat It Two Ways

We're probably reaching a bit with that header, but it sums up very nicely the situation you're in if you focus on gender diversity. What has happened in the past, when the organization was male value-oriented, is that women were forced to compete like men, so they eventually resorted to seeking individual rewards and recognition—just like the men. As a result, the organization lost the advantage of the female view—that the individual benefits most if the whole organization benefits.

If you want to shift your focus and provide women AND men with gender-appropriate rewards you'll have to walk a tricky tightrope. And you'll have to ask yourself what kind of organization you want. You only have three choices:

- *Rewards focused on the success of the individual.*
  This choice repeats the mistakes of history. If you choose this path, the women in your organization are forced to compete like men, and the result is a concentration on personal advantage over organizational gain in the marketplace. Women specializing in promoting the organization in a cooperative way feel unvalued. (Not to mention the risk of having a reputation as a "male bastion" in a society where most of the workers are women.)

- *Rewards focused on the success of the organization as a whole.*
  This choice may seem like the more modern approach, but the results are just the opposite of the first choice. Now you have frustrated males, trying to win, but feeling less victorious when they do.

- *Rewards focused on the success of the individuals AND on the organization as a whole*
  This is the tightrope position. If you take this road you may find yourself pulled from one side to the other. And of course, if you're male-oriented you'll have to fight the unconscious impulse to give male-style rewards, and if you're female-oriented, vice-versa.

Nothing we talk about here is a magic solution. As every manager knows every good plan can be made into bad policy. One organization I know rewards individuals when they want to send a message that someone is valued, and rewards "teams" when they want to send a message that they want the results, but don't want to recognize the individuals responsible. This is very male oriented and a very clear message to the "team builders." This organization considers themselves enlightened, but their turnover among women speaks volumes. When a manager is not convinced that diversity is valuable, the employees figure that out. You can't fool all the people.

What to do? Well, there is a middle ground, but it takes some hard work and serious attention to circumstances. One option is to act as the woman's mentor or, if that's not possible, you can find someone else (the right person) to fill that role. Concentrate on the reward of access and communication. And make a special point of giving the women an opportunity to talk, ask questions, and get feedback. You can even go so far as to ask if you can help (but without implying they are helpless and can't manage without you.) Reward women with time and communication by mentoring or finding mentors for them. And give them the opportunity to talk, ask questions, and get feedback. Be careful not to create an

```
------------------------ Message ------------------------
To: Laura Ricci
From: George Wilkerson
Subject: Tribal Ways

Laura

This whole discussion reminds me of the old Desmond Morris (The
Naked Ape) thing about men being hunters and women being
gatherers. We've got a lot of that metaphor here. If everything
is so tribal, who're the cannibals?

------------------------ Message ------------------------
To: George Wilkerson
From: Laura Ricci
Subject: Tribal Ways

The Competition. The marketplace. Waiting for the moment to gut
the unsuspecting, and carry the spoils off.
```

organizational message that is unintended by not raising the women's visibility just as high as the men's.

And let the men go off and explore; they'll come to you when they've done something and need a double-check. That's when you can give them a trophy. For example, you might engrave a new putter for a special accomplishment, while a woman might appreciate being invited (along with her significant other) out to dinner.

Some managers would argue that the culture of the organization should rule because that is the environment in which the individuals must compete. If folks feel appreciated and dedicated to the work, they rise over the cultural barriers and bring more flexibility to the organization; and some feel the organization and its culture should be promulgated by management.

When that is your organization's attitude, you may need to use our suggestions to suit your situation. If you're in a male oriented firm, you would use male orientation for both men and women, because they both must adapt to that culture to succeed and continue rising in the organization. In a female oriented firm, focus on the group communication (female orientation) because they both must adapt to that culture to succeed and continue rising in the organization.

Unfortunately, in a book like this, we can't address every conceivable permutation. Therefore, we leave you with these general rules (and invite your specific feedback and questions. Just e-mail us at: authors@r-3.com.)

AS A RULE:

- **Give women time to find information prior to beginning a project.**
  Reward this by encouraging them to come to you and then listening and providing answers.

- **Give the trophies to the guys.**
  Let them know that there was competition for the prize. And give them the opportunity to hold it up and show it to the others.

EXERCISE BREAK

You are about to tell two employees about a corporate award they will each be receiving. One is a man, and one is a woman.

- Write a brief statement of how you would phrase the explanation to the woman when you call her into your office so that it has the most value for her.

_____

_____

_____

_____

- Now, write the statement as you would phrase the explanation to the man when you call him into your office so that it has the most value for him.

_____

_____

_____

_____

Answers:

For the man, we'd use words like *Won* and *Beat out*, congratulating him on the specifics that he brought to the award. For the woman, we'd use words like *Accomplished, Built*, and congratulate her on the specifics she helped everyone bring to win the award. Both should be congratulated on the leadership they've demonstrated.

CHAPTER 10

Tears and Beers

J eff thought that being a good manager meant laying everything out on the table. *"I believe in telling it like it is,"* he would say. *"You'll always know what I think because I call a spade a spade."* And he was especially proud of the fact that he treated men and women the same way.

Jeff didn't know that two of his employees, Jack and Sue Ann, were in the midst of divorces from their respective spouses. Both were under a great deal of stress. Jack Merton, a younger energetic man who had moved up quickly, was finishing a difficult year with the firm. The divorce had distracted him often and things hadn't gone well. There had been a number of circumstances where Jack had "dropped the ball." When he called in Jack for the review he didn't pull any punches.

He began by telling Jack that he would not be allowed to interrupt. He also told him that the information he had received about Jack's work habits was unassailable, and there would be no opportunity for questions or explanations. At the end of the review he told Jack that he would not receive a raise and was being placed on probation. He then handed Jack his copy of the evaluation and ushered him out of the office. He didn't notice Jack crumbling up the evaluation and tossing it into the trash as he exited the building.

In the review for Sue Ann, Jeff proved true to his commitment to equality. And she was subjected to a full frontal attack. Nothing was left uncriticized. As he had done with Jack, he told her that she would not be allowed to interrupt or ask questions. And when, at the end, he explained she would not receive a raise and was being placed on probation, she broke down. But this didn't affect his procedure. Rather than offering her a tissue or allowing her to take a break, he continued with his remark, handed her the evaluation, and opened the office door. She left the office humiliated and distressed. And she waited and watched for the opportunity for vengeance.

If a woman cries in the office you can be pretty sure it's one of two things: she's trying to handle anger or trying to ventilate and relieve stress. If a man cries in the office. . . well, when *was* the last time you saw a man crying. . . in the office, or anywhere? Men don't cry. That's not to say they don't get angry or that they don't suffer stress. But they don't handle these circumstances by crying. More than likely, they'll suppress the anger and take it out somewhere else. (Remember. . . Elvis shot his television.)

Most of us are raised to believe that "big boys don't cry," and "young ladies don't fight." When faced with aggressive behavior, boys are taught that it's all right to fight, and girls learn that it's all right to cry. Recognizing and understanding this is the first step toward effectively managing a diverse work force. An effective manager must be able to empathize with the women as well as commiserate with the men.

The Tears Behind the Anger

More than likely, if men were raised to accept crying as an outlet for their anger we'd see a lot more of them crying in their beer. Instead, we see them in the classic "drunken brawls" and "shouting matches." And the media reinforce these "solutions." Despite the clearly detrimental effects of such behavior, it continues to be represented as the way "real men" deal with problems.

```
----------------------- Message -------------------------
To:   Laura Ricci
From:  George Wilkerson
Subject:  Who's in first?

Let me get personal for just a minute.  One of the things I
have had trouble with in my relationships with women is that I
always seem to have difficulty convincing them that I'm on
their team.  When I try to help by offering suggestions for
resolving whatever is wrong, I get attacked.  Is it me, or is
there something in women that causes them to see men somehow as
"the opposition."

----------------------- Message -------------------------
To:  George Wilkerson
From:  Laura Ricci
Subject:  Who's on first?

According to John Gray (the author of "Men are from Mars, Women
are from Venus," the best way to convince women you are on
their side is to comfort them but NOT offer suggestions.  I'd
never realized this before reading his book, but after thinking
about it and trying it out, I agree.

It's not that men are the opposition.  It's that you are
interfering in an important step women take before decision-
making, and that is to talk it out and vent their feelings.
It's as if someone awakens you in the middle of the night,
night after night.  You just want a good night's rest, but they
won't let you have it.  You'd attack THEM too!
```

At the corporate level, we may not see the full-blown bar brawls, but a visit to the local pub reveals a retreat where men can act out the aggression which was stirred up in the office and play giant-killer with their comrades. [When was the last time you heard of a woman who went on a mad shooting spree because she was laid off?]

The Anger Behind the Tears

In contrast with their male counterparts, if women were raised to accept fighting as an outlet for their anger, we'd see a lot more of them in "drunken brawls" and "shouting matches." But women in the workplace face a double bind: they're expected to be able to fight back and they cannot relieve the stress by crying. This ratchets up the pressure, and sometimes the pressure wins.

Women who go to the local pub aren't going there to bad mouth the abusive manager and talk about how they would "kick his butt" if they just had a chance. They go instead to escape. They go to find a listener, an office mate or fellow worker who has suffered as much and will hear out her hurt. The one thing they won't do, though, is talk about solutions.

Doing the Right Thing

A male manager may assume that crying indicates weakness and try to use this to control female employees. He may shame them into doing what he wants by forcing them to withhold their tears. In the same way, he may assume that a male worker who expresses anger has "lost his cool." He may shame the man into repressing his feelings.

Neither of these approaches is constructive or successful. Take this kind of stance and you're setting yourself up for disaster. Eventually, the man and the woman explode. The question is not if, but when. So if you're going to become the type of manager who helps employees manage their stress and deal with their anger in a constructive way you'll need a box of tissues and a punching bag. (Unfortunately, the latter item hasn't become acceptable. . . yet.)

Instead of a bear cave, your office should be seen as a haven. It should not be the corporate equivalent of the vice-principal's office. Employees need to feel secure in the belief that there won't be any retribution for crying or for asking for support when life dishes out more than they can swallow.

Learning to Listen

A manager is not responsible for the personal lives of his or her employees, so you'll need to be careful about what you say. You'll need to present a balanced response—and the responses you give are going to be different depending on gender.

Women in distress most often need to ventilate; nothing more is necessary. They'll be thankful if you just listen. Don't step out of bounds. Don't offer advise. Don't suggest solutions. In fact, because women speak up about personal issues they may resent suggestions for solutions. Once

```
------------------------- Message -------------------------
To:   Laura Ricci
From:  George Wilkerson
Subject:   I was all right...for a while

Laura-

The subject is the opening line of a song you might remember
called "Crying" by Roy Orbison.  I know that most guys feel at
a loss when a woman cries in their presence.  And they are
really lost when another guy does it.  But what about women?
What's *their* reaction to a guy who breaks down and needs the
tissue box?

------------------------- Message -------------------------
To:  George Wilkerson
From:  Laura Ricci
Subject:   You were all right...for a while

Let me think.  Hmmmm...Yes, I've had at least one man cry in my
office.  I handed him the tissue box.  It didn't fluster me.  I
don't recall that I thought anything about it.  (And you guys
think of us as the weaker sex?)
```

they've got some of the worry off their chest, they're free to go back and look for the answer themselves.

Men, on the other hand, expect an answer. They look for solutions. They think that if they study the situation long enough they can find a way to avoid it happening again. And one of the major drawbacks to this is that they may corner themselves. Coming to the conclusion that they have no way out, they may strike out at the perceived aggressor (like a cornered rat) in an explosion of anger. They need to feel secure in the knowledge that they can close the door to your office and blow off steam without ramifications.

Such anger, when felt by women, more often manifests itself through tears. Managers who don't let them vent their anger constructively miss this as an opportunity to treat workplace complaints effectively.

AS A RULE:

- **Don't Assume that Crying Indicates Weakness**
  If she cries? Keep a box of tissue in your office. If all you do is relieve some of the pressure, you automatically increase productivity. If he cries, make sure he feels protected.

- **Encourage the Men to Sound Off**
  Let it be known that they can express their anger freely and in private. And help them find a resolution.

- **Regardless of Gender, Avoid Shame-Based Management**
  Managing by shaming is wasteful and illusory. The rule is simple. Never use shame to manage people. Your mother may have thought it was a good tool, but *she* used it in the kitchen, not the office.

EXERCISE BREAK

A Workplace Evaluation

When you're doing evaluations, each person needs individual attention. Everyone isn't the same. And nowhere is this more apparent than in
work-styles. Leaning on the techniques that match the dominant pattern
of the employee helps your message to be heard.

Almost everyone has elements of both male and female patterns, just
to differing degrees. So both methods have benefit in the workplace. If
you had an all-male crew building a railroad, sharing techniques to improve the results each morning would feel stale pretty fast. If you super-
vise an all female group of telemarketers, waiting to comment on work
well done would feel too late, and would begin to feel like "big brother"
watching over the group.

Here's a checklist to help you the next time you do employee
evaluations:

___ Do you have a box of paper tissues handy?

___ Is the evaluation form completed in ink? (How about showing
up with a penciled-in form and the largest eraser you can find?)

___ Have you honestly defined the purpose of your evaluations? Is
it to document performance or to provide guidance for improvement?

___ If you're documenting performance, do you include ways to
provide guidance for improvement, like commenting on work
well-done (male pattern) or sharing techniques for better work
methods (female pattern)?

CHAPTER 11

When Harry the Dog Meets Sally the Cat

The atmosphere in the shop that afternoon was tense. Barry was miffed at Jerry because he had left work undone the last few nights. Each time, the others could hear Barry grumbling loudly because he had to stay late to finish up.

On Friday, Barry had had enough. As Jerry emptied his coffee cup and reached for his jacket, Barry erupted. Angry words flew between the two men and finally Jerry stormed out of the shop.

Angela, who witnessed the incident, felt stiff from the tension. The confrontation between the two men caused her to, tiptoe around for the rest of her shift. She couldn't wait to escape and go home.

Monday, when Angela arrived, she found Barry and Jerry exchanging jokes and commenting on a television show they had both seen that weekend. She shook her head.

"What's the matter, Angela?" her office partner Don asked.

"Those two should be sorry for what they put us all through," she said. "Here they are yukking it up together as if nothing ever happened."

Don commented that he thought it was great that Jerry and Barry were back to getting along so well.

Angela was confused. "They're all crazy," she thought

Dogs come to work willing and able to perform. They find it easy to leave their personal life outside the door. Cats tend to blend their personal and business lives together—its all an intimate part of them. The cats prefer some distance and independence. The dogs relish their bounding energy; they rush to greet you at the door, and they aren't shy about their dependence for food, exercise and affection.

Every organization needs cats and dogs, and they need the best talents of every breed within the organization. Those managers who harness the best of each breed and incorporate that talent according to the organization's needs will build an organization that is at once solid and elastic, energetic and thoughtful, speedy and deliberate, and willing to take risks.

Fighting like Cats and Dogs

In some respects, men see conflict as a form of battle. The classic idea, "I did it MY way," rests firmly in the back of many men's minds. A dog fight is a battle of equals. It's the term used to describe the classic World War I battle between two aircraft. But a cat fight is fought in an alley. It's dirty, street fighting. This contrast presents the basic difference between the man's and woman's views of conflict. And it highlights the importance of reaching a proper resolution.

To build a successful team, conflict resolution can be an area where women can benefit from adopting the men's way. Cat fights are, quite simply, counterproductive. But you can modify the situation to the woman's advantage. Since you're often in control of the choice of battlefield, the solution is simple and relatively easy to administer. Make sure it's in the open (where everyone can see it) and not in the alley (in the darkness). Take the woman along to witness a conflict AND its resolution.

Simply witnessing the conflict doesn't help. Witnessing the resolution is essential. She has to see the conflict AND its resolution in order to have a method she can adopt. What you're teaching here is twofold: (1) Conflict is sometimes necessary or unavoidable. (2) Resolution is the natural next step.

Strange as it may sound, conflicts between men are *easier* to deal with. Men are taught that conflict is natural and they learn to deal with it early. A man who engages in a conflict is perceived as aggressive and strong, a fighter. It fits right in with the traditional concept of masculinity. Conflicts reaffirm the man's self-image as a warrior and protector. Even if he "loses," as long as he played by the rules, he's seen as having "fought the good fight."

But most often, women don't seem to be able to deal with conflict. It contradicts the traditional concept of femininity. Good little girls don't fight now, do they? Women are taught that conflict is unfeminine. Furthermore, you don't have to learn to deal with conflict if you have someone to protect you. Daddies do that first, and then husbands take over the job. In the past, a woman's biological role as the caretaker of the infants made her vulnerable; she required a protector.

And finally, a woman who engages in a conflict runs the very high risk of being labeled as a "bitch." In a business organization, that label can very quickly cause her to be ostracized, even by other women. (The exact same behavior in a man is readily forgiven; as "aggressive and strong.")

```
----------------------- Message -------------------------
To:  Laura Ricci
From:  George Wilkerson
Subject:  A bit too neat and tidy

Laura, much of this sounds too ideal.  The nature of conflict
is irrational, isn't it?  I think you're asking us to be
terribly rational in the most irrational situations, but I
think that's just not practical.  What do YOU think?

----------------------- Message -------------------------
To:  George Wilkerson
From:  Laura Ricci
Subject:  A bit too neat and tidy

I'm assuming here that the manager is not emotionally engaged
in the conflict; and therefore can be the instructor, standing
at the edge of the conflict and seeing it to successful
resolution.  I guess I DO see it as simply a matter of learning
how to handle the conflict.

As you know, I have a set of stone arches in my office.  They
illustrate the keystone, an engineering accomplishment that
gave the ancient Romans the ability to build large structures
with little support.  But just as important as the keystone is
the fact that the stones are not smooth.  The friction between
them is critical to the structure.  Smooth river rocks could
never hold the same pressure because they would lack the glue
of friction.  I believe that groups avoid lockstep responses to
the marketplace only when they maintain a comfortable amount of
difference or "friction" between members.  The differences are
safeguards.
```

The Yin and Yang in Every Organization

Sometimes, conflict is necessary. At the very least, it's unavoidable. Every organization is bound to have conflict. Those organizations that flourish see a conflict as an indicator of potential trouble, a sign that something needs to be done. It provides a source for identifying problems and often churns up data which can go beyond simply finding a solution. How a manager deals with the conflict is the best indication of the company's health. And when the conflict is between members of the opposite sex, the manager who doesn't understand where each is "coming from" is not as likely to arrive at a useful solution.

To that end, we've been talking about opposites, the yin and yang, cats and dogs, of an organization. Johnson O'Connor's[1] *Objective* personalities and *Subjective* personalities: the Subjectives are the explosive forces which propel the world forward; the Objectives are those who carry it from day to day. Men are rewarded when adopting the former role; women, the latter. But this doesn't mean that they can't reverse roles. Indeed, there are many men who do a great job of "taking care of business" and many women who kick start organizations. In truth, the better view of people (one free of gender) is this one. In the new workforce, there are no men or women, no cats or dogs, no Yin and Yang, only people. And all of these dichotomies are actually facets of the same diamond.

AS A RULE:

- **Whenever possible, take the woman along.**
  Let her witness a conflict AND its resolution.

- **Give people the freedom to float**
  Help them to find their level in relation to everyone else. And make it clear that conflicts generate the glue that holds a team together.

---

[1] Johnson O'Connor Institutes: aptitude testing for career decisions, operating since the 1940's, with offices throughout the U.S.

EXERCISE BREAK

The purpose of this exercise is to watch the process of learning conflict resolution taught by exposure to conflict. You'll need to identify a meeting where you know that conflict and (hopefully) a resolution are likely be played out. Select someone of the opposite sex from within your organization to accompany you to the meeting. When you return, fill out the following chart:

THE CONFLICT (what was it *between*; identify the people and issue(s) involved).

_____

_____

_____

Discuss the conflict with the accompanying person; what was his/her reaction?

_____

_____

_____

In your calendar, make a note once each week for the next three months: Has the accompanying person changed his/her approach to conflict?

Since the purpose of this exercise is to watch the learning process, you shouldn't talk over this topic with your subject after the first discussion. Of course, in the real world, you may need to engage, but if possible just watch and make time regularly to reflect on recent events, watching for change.

100

CHAPTER 12

Good People; Bad Teams

Tom had good results when he was supervising a sales group—
a team of 6 outside sales people. That's the main reason he was
promoted to run the telemarketing group, as well as the fact that
he always seemed to have good ideas and came up with innova-
tive programs.

In his new assignment, he managed 40 telemarketers who represented an important part of the firm's profitability. The
telemarketing group consisted of 37 women and three men, on
two shifts.

Tom had all kinds of ideas for changing the way the group func-
tioned. He also had his eye on some software improvements that
he was convinced would increase productivity.

17 months passed before Tom was moved to another assignment. Production was down and the members of the group were in an uproar. The new software, costing $20,000 had been purchased, but no one was using it. And every one of the new projects Tom designed was tossed away the minute he walked out the door.

While they looked for a replacement for Tom, production climbed back to previous levels—all by itself.

Team building may be the most important skill being taught in organizations today. Recognizing that differences among people enhances the performance of the whole group comes as a revelation to some of the new workforce. The idea that cooperation is more powerful than competition is no news to women, but it comes as a surprise to many men. That's why so many organizations are spending millions to teach just one portion of the workforce that teamwork reaps results greater than the sum of the parts.

This is not to say that all women have gotten it right. Some form cliques in the workplace and when managers notice the cliques formed by women they may wonder if this is the best "team-building" they can hope to accomplish.

A Clique Is Not a Team

Maslow's hierarchy of needs[1] defines five levels: Physiological, Safety, Belonging, Status, and Self-actualization. Cliques operate at the level of belonging. At this stage, the interests and talents of the individual are submerged in order to fit in with a group.

Being in a clique is like being a crawfish in a bucket. Just as one member of the group reaches the top of the bucket and is about to escape, the others reach up and yank him or her back down into the bucket with the rest of them.

You can't have change in groups that are operating at this stage because these groups are not functioning as teams. Dragging a group member back into the bucket may look like teamwork, but it's not. So how can you tell if you have a clique or a functioning team?

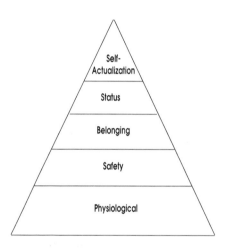

Clique Trap vs Team Work

One of the first signs of the clique is the expulsion of others. Minor infractions become major obstacles for these groups. Discipline is maintained by ostracizing members who step out of bounds. People who are "Movers and Shakers" are always victims of cliques because they don't concentrate on "getting along by going along." If they're agents of change, they won't have an opportunity to make much of a difference because the group can't function in a changing environment. Sameness is a paramount goal.

---

[1]A Theory of Human Motivation by A.H. Maslow from *Psychological Review*, Vol. 50, pp. 370-396, 1943.

```
----------------------- Message --------------------------
To:   Laura Ricci
From:  George Wilkerson
Subject:  Potty Stops
At the risk of getting scatological, I'm wondering if there's a
message in mens and womens rest room visiting behavior.  Women
invariably seem to go to the rest room in pairs.  I think your
comment about there being safety in numbers is valid; women
have to think this way, don't they?  Men don't worry about
being sexually assaulted when they go somewhere.

----------------------- Message --------------------------
To:   George Wilkerson
From:  Laura Ricci
Subject:  Potty Stops

(Gee, George, I had to get a dictionary and look up
scatological.) While women may have some deep-seated
hestitation about being so exposed, I suspect it has more to do
with our social nature.  They are going to the restroom
together to talk about the guys, the meeting, or what to do
next.  Men don't talk about things until they've decided what
they want to do, so a conversation break is not of much
interest.
```

A second sign of the clique is a concentration on group activities like lunches, birthday parties, baby showers, anniversaries, and the like. Individual needs, desires, and interests are submerged in deference to *belonging* to the group. The boundaries between individuals bleeds together as the group hangs out and melds beliefs until, finally, they walk, talk and think alike. During times of crisis or when there's pressure to change, the number of these activities may increase in an effort to "circle the wagons" and keep the group together .

A third sign of the clique is no sign at all; it's simply a lack of change among the players over time. No one can gain weight, lose weight, go back to school, or change their career path without the whole group going along. So when someone learns a new software program or picks up a different skill set they may have difficulty assimilating into a clique because the clique cannot capitalize on differences; it can only submerge them.

So. . . are cliques ever O.K.? Sure. When you have a routine flow of work and need to have everyone adopt the same methods, cliques can be very supportive. If no significant change in the work is anticipated and the work performance is currently at acceptable levels, cliques work for you rather than against you. But the rest of the time, cliques are a problem. They are impediments to change and waste undeveloped talent.

Breaking up (cliques) Is Hard to do

Reorganizing is a great opportunity to break up a clique. The members can be dispersed to different groups. If you can't call for a corporate re-organization, you can break up a clique by permanently removing some members to form a SWAT team for quick action in another part of the organization. Then you can leave them there, or move them to another part of the organization.

Of course, the initial break up will be fought by the members of the clique. And they may enlist others in the organization to politic for their continued existence. So you must be prepared to deal with the Hero or Heroine of the group. They're likely to be strenuous in their objections.

It's High School All Over Again

For girls, cliques are an example of the differences between women and men that's gone bad. Men don't form cliques—at least not in the same way. Because they tend to be more independent and aggressive in seeking their own course, they don't feel the need. (Have you ever wondered why men don't have pajama parties?)

Because they are less convinced that they're career is a dead end, they believe that they can make a difference, so they tend to charge ahead with their own agenda. Women, on the other hand, are more easily convinced that there is "safety in numbers" so they're more comfortable joining groups than men.

AS A RULE:

- **Keep the clique noise level low.**
  If you know you have a clique, make sure the nonproductive restrictions stay at a minimum.

- **If necessary, form a SWAT team.**
  Break up destructive cliques by permanently moving some members to a SWAT team, a special project or assignment.

EXERCISE BREAK

List at least 3 differences between a functioning "Team" and a "clique."

Team	Clique

When you're finished, stand on your head and compare your answers with ours. (If you come up with some we probably forgot, e-mail them to us at: authors@R-3.com.

Team	Clique
Shun close supervision	Respect close supervision
Differences among members are wrestled with	Differences among members are not tolerated
Applauds differences of members	Applauds members who successfully adapt to group mores (dress, behaviour, vocabulary)
Focuses on the individual	Focuses on the group
Individualism is valued and rewarded	Solidarity is valued and rewarded
Relishes dynamic change	Relishes consistency and custom

107

About the Authors

LAURA RICCI is a manager and principal consultant with R³. She works as a marketing manager, trainer and development coach for firms where change demands the best of everyone's energies to succeed. The teams Laura has built for more than a dozen firms in eight industries have all surpassed their previous standards of performance.

Laura attended Golden Gate University, where she earned her M.B.A. and was named Outstanding Graduate of her class. Prior to that, she attended Drake University Law School after working her way through Southern Illinois University at Edwardsville (SIUE). Her classmates at SIUE elected her student body president. She used that opportunity to practice developing dynamic teams and study the methods necessary to endow team members with a pro-active grasp on quality.   http://www.R-3.com

GEORGE WILKERSON has been a manager in academia as well as the business world; he credits his love of the written word as providing the basis for much of his success. He received his B.A. in English from S.U.N.Y at Geneseo and his M.A., also in English, from Syracuse University.

In 1973, after receiving his Ph.D. (in Education) from the University of Texas, he accepted a position as the first Dean of Instruction at the newly founded Austin Community College. In 1980 he went to work as a Project Manager for the Shell Petroleum Corporation and later formed his own consulting firm and publishing company, providing training and documentation services to many small and large firms, including I.B.M., G.E. Corporation, and the United States Coast Guard.

The authors can be reached by email at: authors@R-3.com

Order Form

for

12 Views from Women's Eyes:

Managing the New Majority

Telephone order lines: 1-800-953-6755 open 24 hours a day
or 1-512-288-5005

Fax your order: 1-512-288-5055

Mail your order: *12 Views from Women's Eyes*
c/o Publication Services, Inc.
8803 Tara Lane
Austin, Texas 78737

Order online!:   http://www.R-3.com/bookorder.htm
Please send:

___ copies *12 Views from Women's Eyes:*
Managing the New Majority @ $14.95 each $ _____

Plus $3.95 shipping and handling for the first book   _____

($2.50 for each additional book to the same address)   _____

Plus 8.25% sales tax for books shipped to Texas addresses   _____

TOTAL | $

Name: _____

Address: _____

City _____ State _____ Zip _____

Daytime Phone *(required)*: _____

FAX Phone: _____ Email address: _____

Payment

___ Check *(Please make checks payable to PSI)*

___ Credit Card: ___ VISA   ___MasterCard   ___Discover   ___American Express

Card Number: _____

Expiration Date: _____ Signature: _____

Write to the authors at: authors@R-3.com

Order Form

for

12 Views from Women's Eyes:

Managing the New Majority

Telephone order lines: 1-800-953-6755 open 24 hours a day
or 1-512-288-5005

Fax your order: 1-512-288-5055

Mail your order: *12 Views from Women's Eyes*
c/o Publication Services, Inc.
8803 Tara Lane
Austin, Texas 78737

Order online!: http://www.R-3.com/bookorder.htm
Please send:

___ copies *12 Views from Women's Eyes:*
Managing the New Majority @ $14.95 each $ _____

Plus $3.95 shipping and handling for the first book   _____

($2.50 for each additional book to the same address)   _____

Plus 8.25% sales tax for books shipped to Texas addresses   _____

TOTAL $ _____

Name: _____

Address: _____

City _____ State _____ Zip _____

Daytime Phone *(required)*: _____

FAX Phone: _____ Email address: _____

Payment

___ Check *(Please make checks payable to PSI)*

___ Credit Card: ___ VISA   ___MasterCard   ___Discover   ___American Express

Card Number: _____

Expiration Date: _____ Signature: _____

Write to the authors at: authors@R-3.com